What

M000083341

"Elise Katch has written a gripping and powerful account of her internal process as she sought a Jewish divorce *(get)*. Once I started reading it, I couldn't put it down. Katch combines personal reflections on the process itself with a compelling, self-revealing account of her own inner life. One feels that one is participating in a consciousness-raising group, and inevitably Katch forces the rest of us to come to grips with our own experiences of Jewish ceremonies and our own process of detaching from relationships that no longer work. It is precisely her intensely personal revelations that make this book work, and paradoxically make it most universal. This is a book that will contribute to spiritual and psychological reawakening, a powerful tool of spiritual renewal."

—**Michael Lerner**
editor of *Tikkun* magazine and
author of *The Politics of Meaning*

"Elise Katch's *The Get* is a story of one woman's search for truth and justice in the midst of a painful divorce. A surprising glimpse into the hidden and often misunderstood world of Jewish Orthodoxy, Ms. Katch's unflinching examination of her own grief, anger and ultimate triumph is a deeply moving book."

—**Ed Stein**
award-winning editorial cartoonist
with the *Rocky Mountain News* and creator
of the cartoon strip *Denver Square*

"Elise Katch writes from a profound experience. She, a therapist, underwent the process and describes it eloquently and with heart. Many others in her place seeking to free themselves from their spousal entanglement would want to see how she scouted the territory for them. She experiences 'the full catastrophe' and in retrospect is glad. Magnificent read."

—**Rabbi Zalman Schachter-Shalomi**
author of *From Age-ing to Sage-ing*

"*The Get* is a love story—unique, painful, wonderful. A spiritual and emotional journey of loving—by letting go."

—**Dr. Carla Garrity**
author of *Caught in the Middle*

"*The Get* is a highly original and important contribution to our understanding of the personal impact of divorce. Elise Katch has captured with exquisite sensitivity the poignancy, longing and loss suffered in divorce. She has done so with compelling tenderness, thoughtfulness and forgiveness. Anyone contemplating a divorce should read this powerful personal account of one person's journey on the path to divorce. This is an important book for men as well as women."

—Honorable Leland P. Anderson
District Court Judge, Jefferson County, Colorado

"*The Get* is a powerful story about letting go. Katch fascinates her reader with the intersection of ancient tradition, modern sensibility and timeless human experience. This book is filled with the special wisdom born of living through divorce with eyes and heart open."

—Rabbi Tirzah Firestone
author of *With Roots in Heaven*

"The ending of a marriage is a painful event, and Elise Katch eloquently describes her personal loss and mourning in *The Get*. The role of the Jewish divorce process and the *get* as a powerful healing tool is an important theme in the book. . . . Rabbis, lawyers, judges, family therapists, mediators and Jewish community leaders would do well to read this book in order to appreciate the positive role a *get* can play in enabling the parties to get on with their lives after a divorce."

—Sharon Shenhav
attorney and director of the International Jewish
Women's Human Rights Watch

"A fast, well-written and wonderful read! An intensely personal memoir of a soul-searching, meaningful experience. A book to be read by all men and women, Jew and non-Jew, to develop insight into the role of the *get*. The author recounts pain, coping, survival and healing as she experienced life-changing events. Reading this book gives one an intense understanding of divorce, healing and the process worked through."

—Joyce D. Miller
past president of the Coalition of Labor Union Women and
past vice president of the AFL-CIO

the GET

A SPIRITUAL MEMOIR
OF DIVORCE

Elise Edelson Katch

SiMCHA
PRESS
An Imprint of Health Communications, Inc.®

Deerfield Beach, Florida
www.simchapress.com

Library of Congress Cataloging-in-Publication Data

Katch, Elise Edelson, date.
    The get : a spiritual memoir of divorce / Elise Edelson Katch.
        p.   cm.
    ISBN 1-55874-929-2 (pbk.)
    1. Divorce—Religious aspects—Judaism. 2. Katch, Elise Edelson,
    date—Marriage. 3. Katch, Elise Edelson, date—Divorce.
    4. Spiritual life—Judaism. I. Title.

BM713.5 .K38 2001
296.4'444—dc21

                                 2001020959

Simcha Press, its Logos and Marks are trademarks of Health Communications, Inc.

Publisher: Simcha Press
               An Imprint of Health Communications, Inc.
               3201 S.W. 15th Street
               Deerfield Beach, FL 33442-8190

Ketubah on cover designed by Samson Margolis; courtesy of Aaron and Dorothy Margolis
Cover design by Andrea Perrine Brower
Inside book design by Dawn Grove

For Kaiya

daughter, teacher, mirror, friend

As a little kid I was fascinated by cowboy movies. There always seemed to be one scene where the good guy gets bitten by a rattlesnake. Another cowboy rides along, gets off his horse, takes out a knife and slices several cuts through the snake wound. He then places his mouth on the rattlesnake bite and sucks out the venomous poison. That scene remained in my consciousness long before I understood *metaphor*.

When a man taketh a wife, and marrieth her, then it cometh to pass, if she find no favour in his eyes, because he hath found some unseemly thing in her, that he writeth her a bill of divorcement, and giveth it in her hand, and sendeth her out of his house.

Deuteronomy 24:1

The very altar weeps for one who divorces the wife of his youth.

Talmud Gittin 90b

CONTENTS

ACKNOWLEDGMENTS

Making *The Get* a reality could not have been possible without those who read the manuscript at various stages or were there with a simple ear to listen. Friends became the glue that held me—and the manuscript—together.

The Get could never have been written without the love and encouragement of my incredible daughter, Kaiya Katch. She is truly a unique instructor of life whose wisdom keeps me on the right path. Thank you, dearest Kaiya, for your constant affirmations and presence in my life. I am blessed beyond words.

Rabbi Zalman Schachter-Shalomi suggested that I

write about the *get*. There simply would be no manuscript had he not believed in me. Thank you, Reb Zalman, for your special guidance, love and encouragement.

Rabbi Mordecai Twerski exhibited unique sensitivity and unlimited time for me. Thank you, Reb Twerski, for your concern, emotional support and acceptance.

Rabbi Michael Lerner: Thank you, Michael, for your wonderful words of praise and love. Thank you also to Rabbi Tirzah Firestone for your invaluable friendship.

I could not have made it through the dark times without the unconditional love and support of my remarkable sister, Judy Goldberg, and her husband, Bill. And thanks to JoAnn Ross, my dearest friend, who *always* had time to listen with a compassionate ear. Such special people. Thank you for being there.

From the very beginning, Carla Garrity encouraged me to seek publication and never ceased to provide kind words of support. Judi Wolf was extremely enthusiastic in her belief in *The Get*, as was Nancy Gary. Also, Judge Leland Anderson was encouraging at just the right moment. Thank you all so much for your support at a critical time.

Special thanks to Gary Lozow, a longtime friend who was consistently there. Thanks also to the greatest friend, Hil Margolin, with his regular calls, "How are you—

really?" Many thanks to Bill Redak, who continued to be understanding—no matter what. And there are no words to describe my dear friend, Paul Zweig, and his endless love and availability. Thank you, guys.

Many thanks to my newfound friend, Kristen Diesel— my snowboard bud, who actually thinks I'm fun to be with. And Mary Beth Anderson, who understands when I fall through the cracks. Thank you, Sarah Goldberg, for your love and friendship. And thanks to Gary Dragul, who was just there in a special way. Thank you, Margaret Hoeppner, for being a lasting friend. Thank you to the greatest Outward Bound instructor—Chris Roberts. He believed in me. And thanks to Nigel Bell, Hobey Oliveira and Patty McPherson, who never complained, but showed me love and compassion. And thanks also to Gordon Miller, who took the time when he had no time.

Several families were there continuously and deserve special appreciation: The family of Alan, Janet, Rachel and Reuben Brandt. The family of Ed Stein and Lisa Hartman and Gabe and Tasha Hartman Stein. Thank you, guys, for loving me and putting up with me. The family of Chuck, Robyn and Mollie Jacobs—who provided me an invaluable home for the holy days—and, of course, thanks to Carl and Fran Jacobs. The family of Hil and

Denys Margolin and Ben and Lilli, who allowed me to invite myself over—no questions asked. The family of Burt and Robin Siegelman and Bryn, Ryan and Shane, who *always* made me feel accepted and loved.

Also thanks to the special families of Dan and Joy Wilhelm, Fred and Margaret Hoeppner, Brad and Michelle Goldberg, Steve and Deanne Kapnik, Michael Kinzer and Chris Jobin, Ed Abraham and Norma May Isakow, David and Debra Flitter, Jeff and Shira Reiss, Michael and Sandy Melvoin, Jim and Judy Brantz, David and Carrie Danz, Daniel and Diane Gardner, and Ron, Rachael and Mia Deprey. Just knowing you were there carried me through to the "other side."

Over the years of writing *The Get,* I have had endless manuscript readers. Thanks to all: Kathy Borgen, Lisa Johnson, Anne Stern, Susan Bruton, Bonnie Dannen, Jen Hannen, Jill Wheeler, Sydney Harriet, Krista Hoeppner, Jim Berger, Daisy Berl, Sari Horovitz, Chaz Ebert, Randi Gelfand, Tere Britton, Jim Heiser, Linda Jankovsky, Othniel Seiden, Dennis Britton, Dona Mandell, Megan Garrity, Sarah Brenner, Leigh Baker and Marsha Gelfand.

Thank you to many others who helped in special ways: Meir Mark, Art Frazin, Leslie Mitchell, Harris Sherman,

Stanley Stefancic, Michael Axelrad, Beverly Schumacher Bodman, Susan Berson, Bobby Morris, Joe Garner, Marilyn Atler, Steve Berson, Chuck Snyder, Ellyn Hutt, Pixie Campbell, Stephen Cohen, Ruth Snyder, Miriam Ginsberg, Bob Hoffman, Alice Silverberg, Bob LaCrosse, Charles Goldstein, David Sanders, Norm Brownstein, Susan Heitler, Mabel Graft and Barbara Wagner.

And thanks to those who might not even know they played a part in this vast endeavor: Ora Zipper, Amy Mills, Barbara Hyatt, Frank McKibben, Nora Schrutt, Nama Frenkel, Randall Shelton, Phyllis Knight, Ingrid Slezak, Ann Blaugrund, Diane Pincus, Loraine Friend, Erika Ross Norman, Paul Wexler, Ginny McKibben, Sam Sloven, Karen McDowell, Marion Gottesfeld, Paul Schadler, Beth Seligman, Hank Canham, Janet Mules and Marlene Zweig.

Thank you to the kids (now young adults) who provided emotional support and were an unwritten part of this story: Andrew Todd, Chris Cook, Meredy Martin, Whitney McMurtry, Anne Williams Elmquist, Holly Shaw and Catherine Wilhelm.

I wish to deeply thank the families and individual patients I have worked with professionally over the years. I have learned greatly from you as I sit appearing so confident with my *therapist* look. (Trevor accuses me of that look.) Actually, I am in awe of *your* strength and courage.

The Ketubah on the cover was designed by Samson Margolis. I would like to thank his son, Aaron, and Aaron's wife, Dorothy, for their permission to use this wonderful marriage contract. Thank you to the folks at the Hoffman Institute and the Landmark Forum who helped me to create unlimited possibilities. And thank you to Congregation Kohelet for allowing me the vehicle to explore my spirituality with freedom, depth and acceptance.

Thank you to Peter Vegso for gathering together an incredible publishing staff. Special thanks to Tom Sand at Health Communications, who had early faith in my writing. Exuberant thanks to all of the people at Health Communications who said "yes" to *The Get*. I am grateful for the tireless efforts and support of my compassionate editor, Susan Tobias, and publicist, Kim Weiss, at Simcha Press who honored the integrity of the manuscript. There would be no "book" without you two. Thanks to Heath Lynn Silberfeld for teaching me the difference between "was" and "were." Thanks to the folks in the art department for their extra effort—Larissa Hise Henoch, Andrea Perrine Brower and Dawn Grove. And to everyone at

Health Communications—if one could script a publisher, you all would be it. You're the best.

And, of course, love to my parents, Betty and Alan Edelson, who gave me an unending appreciation for the written word. I am sure you guys are watching all of this— with pride and a huge smile.

AUTHOR'S NOTE

I really believe *The Get* came from another place—certainly another time. As I read through many passages that I penned, no memory existed of the actual writing. I sometimes asked, "Where *were* these words coming from?"

The events described in *The Get* were culled from memory, which does not always have the accuracy of a photograph. Some of the experiences might not have happened exactly as written, but they represent my mental record. If the words have offended or hurt *anyone,* I sincerely apologize.

It must be noted also that many of the names of living persons have been changed.

When anger between parents continues long after the divorce has become final, the children are left with indelible wounds. Parents may heal and move on to new lives, but children carry the bruises into their own adult relationships. Divorce is a parental choice. It should not be an *eternal* gift to our children. What is so simple is that it does not have to be.

A ceremony (such as the *get*), which marks the end of a marriage, should be encouraged no matter what religious belief exists. A *recipe* for divorce, as presented in *The Get,* would certainly help to sever the relationship cord, and thus diminish the endless anger that negatively binds these couples together for eternity.

It is my wish that those who are in good solid relationships will learn from the experience of *The Get* and say to themselves, "I will never go down that road." I want *The Get* to be a deterrent for those who believe that divorce will provide an *easy* resolution. I would also like *The Get* to be an affirmation for those who have struggled and maintained successful relationships. And lastly, I hope *The Get* will provide a template for those ending relationships, but wishing to heal and grow from the loss. Transformation to an improved existence *is* possible.

INTRODUCTION

His eyes showed concern. He said that we needed to talk.

"I don't want you hurt by the process. You should be healed and separate."

I have to say I was surprised by his intensity and choice of words.

> *This is very important.*
> *I want the get to be good for you.*
> *It is a powerful experience.*

On some obscure level I already knew this. I can't tell you why, but for a long time I sensed that the *get*, this unique Jewish divorce, the one my husband was so anxious to complete, was something very special.

Part I

Before the *Get*

1

Another Woman

Almost immediately after our separation, my husband began to spend serious time with a woman I knew. A professional acquaintance of mine. Someone I liked. We had recently spent a great weekend together, and when she called, on that first night after the retreat, I thought it was to make plans for dinner or a movie.

"I think your husband is going to ask me out," she said on the telephone. "We met at services, and I really want to know what you think because it doesn't seem like you and I can remain friends if we begin to date."

Date?
The word jolted me.
It was too soon.
And . . .

After our special weekend together, I was excited at the
thought of a new friend. Friends were worth a lot these
days. A lifeline to continuation. They kept you above water
when the predominant feeling was drowning. She and I had
just spent three days together pouring our hearts out about
lengthy marriages and recent separations. During the
annual religious women's retreat, we turned a casual relationship into a bonded experience. There was a definite
connection. We talked about my husband, our relationship
and what kind of a person he was. I shared things with her
that I had told no one. She seemed so interested.

Her pain was obvious during our weekend together, as
she also shared details of her failed marriage. She wanted to
know what I thought about the woman her husband was
dating.

"How could he fall in love so soon? We have only been
separated two months. If I hear one more person tell me
how wonderful she is, I'll scream."

I knew the woman her husband was dating and I liked

her. Without much thought I said, "Better her than some bimbo."

"A bimbo would be easier on the ego."

I did not agree.

I know I wasn't thinking clearly when I responded to her telephone call, as I told her that I honestly believed that dating my husband would be okay. Denver was such an incestuously small community. It seemed understandable that she and my husband found each other. They were both lonely and newly separated, with thirty-year marital histories. I thought it was good that I liked her. I was just unprepared for my husband to begin to date. After all, we were *just separated*. I had no plans for them to fall in love.

I didn't know much about my husband's life. At his suggestion we had little contact. So strange. One day there exists a powerful connection. Assumptions of forever. Then nothing. This was not like our previous separation when I had asked him to leave.

I asked him to move out. We needed distance. His rage was simply too intense, and it frightened our daughter. I never thought of it as abusive. It was just the way things were. It surprised me that I felt an immediate sense of relief when he left. My husband's experience was different. The aloneness was intolerable for him. We had contact several times a week. I complained.

"Isn't this about distance? We talk and spend more time together now that we are separated."

During that first separation, he called often at two or three in the morning. "I need you. I love you. Help me through this terrible night. Please."

I eased him through those awful times. I never thought of telling him not to call. He was in too much pain. This was a time to work things out. It was not punishment. Now, two years later, *this* separation felt very different.

He moved out the day before I flew to Chicago. I thought about not going. A celebration seemed alien at this moment, but staying home seemed wrong.

Over the years, my sister and I had supported each other during our children's significant life experiences. There

wasn't much family left, and we were sisters. Her significance in my life was not simply about sharing genetic matter. She was someone very special to me. Not going felt too
self-indulgent.

The event in Chicago was my niece's high school
graduation from Latin. The fat acceptance envelope from
Amherst had arrived a few weeks earlier, making this
graduation weekend a very special celebration. Most certainly a time to be happy.

It seemed terribly self-centered to hand my niece a
graduation present, give her a big hug and then tell everyone that my husband just moved out. No one expected him
to attend the graduation. He never liked our trips to the
Windy City. So I decided to tell no one about the empty bed
waiting for me at home. This was a time reserved for joy.

As happy as I was for my sister and her special family, I
have to say that the weekend was really hard for me. Three
glorious days of celebration seemed to accentuate my loss
and arouse feelings of jealousy. This new sensation frightened me, as envy was an emotion to which I never related.

The source of my feelings did not arise from material possessions, such as beautiful homes with magnificent lake views.
This coveting was about family and everything I had taken
for granted and accepted as a given. Suddenly, the simple act

of sitting down to pancakes and eggs while discussing the day's plans seemed luscious. Sadness overwhelmed me as I thought about the possibility of a future defined by a fragmented family. Leaving Chicago was not going to be easy.

He was a law student, I was an elementary school teacher. We had no money. None of our friends had money. It didn't seem to matter. I don't remember wanting a whole lot. It was the sixties. In those days my wardrobe consisted of two pairs of Levi cords, one or two skirts (my uniform at work), a couple of turtlenecks, a sweater and desert boots.

Our parents helped. My husband's mom paid for law school. My parents paid for my dental work. With that assistance, the income from my teaching salary, even though it was quite small, was enough.

The cost of living was not very high and money never seemed to be a real concern. We drove one car—a light-blue squareback Volkswagen—and gasoline cost twenty-five cents a gallon. We lived a simple existence. Our life was pretty uncomplicated and, of course, we were in love.

We paid $125 a month (including utilities) for a one-bedroom apartment at the Logan House. Our neighborhood, Capitol Hill, didn't have a good reputation, but we never thought of ourselves as poor. The $2 Chinese dinners at the Lotus Room never felt like a sacrifice.

After one year of marriage, we almost bought a beautiful Tudor-style two-story brick home at 19th and Niagara. The neighborhood was changing (people of color were moving across Montview), and prices were low. The elderly owner wanted $17,000.

We loved the house and thought that living in an integrated neighborhood was a great idea. After all, it had only been a year since we were in Boulder holding hands and singing "We Shall Overcome" with James Farmer. Those were the days of freedom riders and Selma.

If we bought the house we could afford the monthly payment of $142, but if the furnace or dishwasher broke we could not absorb the additional expense. As much as we wanted that wonderful house, we passed on the opportunity to buy. The possibility of financial pressure frightened us.

We never lived beyond what we could afford. We paid cash for everything. It was our tenth year of marriage before I had my first credit card. I paid the full balance each month, never understanding the meaning of "finance charge." Our parents taught us well. Money was pretty much a nonissue in our lives.

As I walked through the Denver airport concourse on my way home, ripe with thoughts of my sister and her family, I became consumed with emptiness. A cold chill came upon me as I imagined my daughter's graduation the following year from Manual High School. Reflecting upon the past few days of celebration in Chicago, I wondered whether our daughter would sit between her parents at graduation dinner.

Why didn't we talk about this before he packed his bags and walked through the door? Had we really thought about what it would be like for our daughter? Or did we assume "She's older, she can handle it"? The separation toyed with something precious—our family.

While moving slowly through the airport, my eyes fixed on couples and families. Children running to parents. Wives greeting husbands. Boyfriends standing with a single rose. It was like being pregnant and noticing for the first time that the world was filled with children. This became a slow, excruciating walk as my eyes caught a paired, coupled world.

Intense
overwhelming aloneness
and
disconnection
from
the world I knew.

The train at the airport became a metaphor of transformation. The jingle over the speaker system that always sounded a bit like Las Vegas, and the voices of journalists Reynelda Muse and Pete Smyth, would never be the same again. I returned to Denver a very different person.

As the taxi pulled away from the curb at our home, *Bellaire*, I realized my daughter was away for the evening. Nothing strange about that. She was at the age, developmentally, when parents were not exactly favored companions.

Our timing for a separation was not exactly great either. This was not going to help our daughter as she began the rigorous college application process. Competition for good schools was fierce. She worked hard in high school and set her sights high. It was good that she didn't have to worry about college money—a promise from her father. The pressure to maintain grades in advanced placement classes was intense. Now when she needed a solidness around her, the world as she knew it was being altered drastically.

My daughter and I had always been close, but now she was, appropriately, pulling away and establishing her own life. I did not expect her to greet me at the door with "Hi, Mom. Let's order pizza, and you can tell me about your weekend."

It probably was her plan not to be home when I arrived from Chicago. As much as she loved my sister and her family, I don't think she was interested in hearing about the wonderful graduation weekend. I understood. Her previously secure world was crumbling and now being defined by uncertainty and fear. In her reality, listening to stories about happy families wasn't exactly therapeutic.

Selfishly though, on this watershed evening, I wished my adolescent daughter were at home. Even if she were not exactly excited to see me, I simply needed a hug and some companionship. This was strange, as generally I loved my time alone.

On this particular spring night . . .
I wanted to be anywhere but alone at *Bellaire*.

2

What Is This *Get*?

Our turquoise-blue front door was always a welcome sight as I returned from trips. I loved this great house. So comforting. The perfect place for carving out sacred alone time. But not tonight. The aloneness and the emptiness on this evening were unsettling. Even Max, our spectacular black-and-white springer spaniel was gone, spending the weekend with my husband.

Why hadn't I thought about this moment? It would have been nice to have seen his tail racing at hummingbird speed, to watch that slow stretch as he moved out of his kennel and to have heard those great welcome-home sounds.

Max. Special dog that I could exercise by getting to chase
the beam of light from a flashlight. I thought of his passion
for tennis balls, not pheasant. He never became the great
hunter, as planned. But he was a wonderful companion.

I used to think that his problem was being too smart. But
Kevin Fitzgerald would always tease, "Yeah, Max—he's not
exactly a rocket scientist."

I walked from the curb toward our front door, thinking
how beautiful the flowers looked this year. You could see
them clearly because of the intense moon. I paused for a
moment before turning the key and pushing down on the
front door latch. I wasn't so sure that I wanted to move
through the doorway.

The house was dark but I closed the front door without
turning on any lights. I quickly dropped my luggage in the
entryway and ran up the stairs. Without a thought, I
grabbed frantically for the telephone. I had to call my
husband.

Now I was the one alone with the terror, reaching out. I
needed him to help me through this night.

We had to talk. It was important. We needed to think

about this thing we seemed to be doing so callously without any real thought. Did he see the path we were careening down? Did he understand the *forever* consequences?

After thirty years of being together, I didn't want to live my life alone, shopping at King Soopers on Saturday night and thumbing through the personals. I loved my life. I loved my family. Our daughter deserved two caring parents sitting next to each other when she marched down the aisle at her graduation.

> We needed
> to
> think this
> thing
> through.

Our parting a few days earlier had been amiable. He had told me to have a good time in Chicago. We laughed as he suggested buying me a new car for a separation present. My Audi Quattro was causing me to develop a personal relationship with my mechanic. Frequent visits to the shop suggested that I was going to need a new car. And after all the

"D" word had never been thought about or even mentioned. We were just separated. Until we worked things out.

I grabbed for the telephone, pulling it off the nightstand, and dialed my husband's number. As I waited forever to hear his voice, I remembered his frantic, desperate calls in the middle of the night, when he was so very alone. I remembered how I comforted him. And then I thought again. This is just temporary. We were laughing together a few days ago. He's still my friend.

"How was the graduation?" he asked.

"It was wonderful."

"That's nice," he said.

I took a deep, frantic breath.

"I want to see you—maybe tonight? I really need to talk to you. It's really important. I think we need to get together."

I waited for his response. But what followed was the longest pause.

"I can't do that," he answered. "My psychiatrist told me that I have to stay away from you. We can't see each other. You're not good for me." He must have said good-bye. I do not remember anything else.

In the dark, I sat on the edge of the bed, unable to hang up the phone. I must have believed that if I held on to the receiver a bit longer, my husband would return with a different response.

The shrieking stutter of the telephone line startled me as tears stung my face. I don't know how long I remained without thought or breath in the statuelike position. Time simply stopped.

I stood up, walked to the bathroom, splashed some cold water on my face and took a breath from deep inside. The empty feeling of abandonment penetrated my unsteady limbs. I had to find some way to keep my soul intact, as I watched my essence leave my body. So strange. I did not understand. What did he mean? We said vows. We made promises. To each other and to God.

I called my best friend, who lives in Aspen. She was the only one (besides my daughter) who knew of the separation. It didn't feel right telling others before I told my sister, who was still celebrating. I refused to spoil her joy.

My friend and I talked for awhile. I told her about the graduation and the call to my husband. Just talking to her made me feel better.

"Why does it hurt so much?" I asked.

Because it's over.

As her words throbbed in my veins and pierced my soul, I realized that I had not accepted, nor even thought about, the possibility of an end. In my mind our situation was simply a transition period, until we were together again.

My relationship with my Aspen friend predated both of our marriages. We met when I was still a college student at Colorado University in Boulder.

Our friendship had weathered my immaturity and self-centeredness. She remained a good friend during her pregnancy, even after I suggested she read *Rosemary's Baby*.

"I have no intention of falling into that game of choosing sides. I love you both," she would say with a smile.

Several months into the separation, legal work took my husband to Aspen. His trial lasted a few days and ended conveniently on Friday. As his stay continued into the weekend, he spent some time with my good friend. Over breakfast he told her about the new woman in his life. He shared how much in love he was and how good things were between the two of them.

"I never knew it could be this simple," he said.

"He's really happy," my friend related to me. "And he looks so good."

I don't have an explanation for how things got to this point. I should, but I don't. Let's call it sleepwalking. We never really talked about getting divorced. It just became a given. He fell in love and came to believe that in order to be happy I needed to be out of his life. We had a mediator and two attorneys, and then the process became a reality, with an agenda of its own.

Once we began negotiations with attorneys, our communication deteriorated quickly. Any kind of civil interaction that previously existed simply vanished. Money became the central and only issue. For two people who had never once in thirty years together argued about money, this was a shock. My husband had been such a generous person. Now he was telling me that there was no education money for our daughter who was busy applying to prestigious eastern colleges.

He seemed uncomfortable that I maintained a good relationship with the woman he was dating. She and I understood that friendship made good sense, and besides, she was very good to my daughter. That meant a great deal to me. We both knew the best situation was simply for everyone to be nice to each other. We understood deeply that conflict and continued fighting between parents devastated children.

"Stay away from her, and stay away from me," he said one evening on the telephone, making it clear that he wanted no contact outside of our formal divorce negotiations.

The harsh reality of our deteriorating relationship only caused difficulty and pain for our daughter as she apprehensively prepared for her special graduation weekend. *Not fair,* I thought to myself. *Why can't we just sit together—for her?*

My daughter's graduation from high school should have been an occasion filled with joy, but it was not. From the corner of my eye I watched a tearful graduate pretend. Surrounded by her friends, I caught an attempt to smile. Her father was the only parent not present at the graduation dinner.

He must have believed that he had a good reason for not attending the celebration of friends and families, but the result was that our daughter became a receptacle for toxic emotions. It was so wrong, so hurtful and so unnecessary. This was *her* time to celebrate achievement, not ache over the disintegration of her family.

It shakes you to the core when someone you have shared your life with suddenly responds to you as though you are a clerk at the motor vehicle bureau.

Correspondence was now signed "Sincerely yours."

Angry messages

on my

> voice mail
> cold unfeeling letters
> unkept promises
> and
> avoidance.

My new reality disturbed me, as I came to understand the depth of his anger. I kept thinking that someone I did not know was fueling his negative emotions. I learned to relate to a very different being. My husband had rapidly become a stranger. This was not the same person I walked with in the autumn wind.

Given the lack of communication and the intensity of his feelings, his first friendly telephone call to me specifically requesting a Jewish dissolution, a *get*, seemed odd.

I had not yet made the connection between his intimate relationship with a new woman and his urgent requests specifically for a Jewish disconnection.

"Let's talk about the *get*," he suggested. "How about next week?" he asked. "The scribe will be in town. You don't even have to be there. It's no big deal. It only takes a few minutes."

I received calls like this on a fairly regular basis, and they confused me. I was not sure of exactly what he wanted and I did not always understand everything he said. Given his persistence, I had to wonder. How could the *get*, this Jewish ending, be *no big deal* when he appeared so eager for its completion?

If this had been normal time, I would have drawn upon my strength and knowledge in order to remain focused. But separation and divorce altered the time continuum and sapped one of the very wisdom that was needed to survive. I was not functioning in a smart way. Unbalanced was the predominant feeling. Like walking on talus with a fifty-pound pack.

According to Rabbi Joseph Telushkin, a Jewish scholar, the Torah (the first five books of the Hebrew Bible) is considered Judaism's central document. It contains 613 commandments, which form the backbone of Jewish law. But in all of the Torah there is just one verse on the subject of divorce. The phrase "and he shall write her a bill of divorcement" is the origin for the Jewish divorce, the *get*.

I knew the *get* was an Orthodox experience, an ancient

ritual marking the end of a Jewish marriage. Difficult to grasp, it was both process and thing—both ceremony and document.

> The *get* then
> becomes
> both
> an event
> and
> a written record.

A friend sent me a *New York* article about a man who refused to give his wife a *get*. The civil divorce had been final for quite a while, but the husband did not grant the Jewish dissolution. In doing this—in refusing to go through the process of writing the *get*—he was able to stop his former wife from marrying again.

Even after a finalized civil divorce, remarriage is not allowed without a sanctioned *get*. In the eyes of God, it is believed both husband and wife remain connected through the original marriage vows. Obtaining a *get* thus becomes critical in the process of remarriage.

❧ ❧ ❧

For some reason unknown to me, there seemed to be a great deal of interest in my specific encounter with the *get*. Whenever someone heard about my marital situation, a question followed immediately: "Are you going to do a *get*?" Talking about the process began to feel like sailing uncharted waters in the midst of a rediscovered ancient ocean.

At the annual women's retreat I was approached by a dear woman friend, a Boulder rabbi named Tamar. Our time together was always special, and on this day, as usual, we had only a few precious moments together. With genuine concern, she asked how I was, and if I was prepared to do the *get*.

"Do you understand what is involved?"

In a short time she conveyed to me that the process of obtaining a *get* could be difficult—even humiliating.

"Be careful," she said. "Take care of yourself."

I came to understand her reasons for concern when I discovered that the giving and receiving of the *get* took place in the presence of a *beit din,* a rabbinical court.

The two of us
and
men in black
ending our connection.
Dark visions in
one room together
yet
separate and
alone.

    The ultra-Orthodox existence seemed rigid and foreign, alien to my thinking and somewhat frightening. In the world I lived in I had more close friends who were Catholic than ultra-Orthodox.

    In the presence of Orthodox men, I felt unsure of myself. Maybe it was because I never seemed to understand the rules and I felt like an outsider. When I was in the presence of Orthodox men, self-conscious thoughts dictated. I felt less than what I was, as perpetual questions rattled my thoughts and altered my consciousness. *Is my skirt long enough? Should my head be covered? Do I say the blessing now? Is it sundown yet? Can you see my eyes?*

I always felt judged. And it unbalanced me to be around men who would not shake my hand. I understood that Orthodox men and women who were not married were not allowed to touch. I accepted that version of Judaism as a different way, and I had great respect for many spiritual leaders who followed that path. But Orthodoxy was not my way.

I liked men
too much.

I must tell you how odd it is simply to be talking about Orthodoxy, because for at least half of our marriage we didn't observe any Jewish ritual. We did not affiliate with a synagogue or participate in services—not even during the High Holy Days of Rosh Hashana and Yom Kippur.

But after the sixties we did entertain the idea of becoming religious. It seemed to be a natural progression. Many folks were following Jim Morrison to the "other" side. During that unsettled, curious time, it seemed as though everyone was looking for more.

3

Filling the Void

Many years have passed since we first considered the possibility of living an observant life. At the time it was never more than a passing thought. The chasm between "Light My Fire" and "Ma Toh Vu" was too great. Observance of simple commandments was difficult; my husband even struggled with wearing a *kippah* (head covering) while studying the Torah.

This was a time to join a counterculture group like the Weathermen—not a temple. A time to be irreverent—to stretch the confines of established society. It was a painfully rebellious time—Temple Ball hash, Yasgur's farm, Kent State, Nixon, My Lai. A time to break the rules, not to observe them.

A few years out of law school my husband began to study Torah with a young professional Orthodox man. After several weeks, this teacher invited us to his home for Friday night dinner. He lived in a religious community on the other side of town, the west side.

In my childhood home, Friday nights were not religious but they always felt special. This was the night my mother made her incredible soup. We ate together as a family and watched on TV, *I Remember Mama* and the *Gillette Friday Night Fights*. Rocky Marciano and chicken soup.

When we accepted the dinner invitation, I had no concept of Shabbat, the Jewish Sabbath. Friday nights were movie nights for us—a box of popcorn and an evening at the Esquire or the Ogden.

For me, reaching each of my thirty-five sixth-grade students every day was challenging and exhausting work, not to mention the daily after-school and evening work that went along with the job.

I don't think my students were unique, but they never seemed excited about common denominators or Latin American capitals. What they wanted came at the end of the day—someone to talk to. And many of them weren't interested in ever going home. Henry Kempe had not yet raised our consciousness.

My husband was working at Denver Legal Aid. His caseload was overwhelming, and by the end of the week exhaustion and frustration with the system were evident. "Initiation by fire," he always used to say.

He never talked much about his work, but I do remember one specific case. A client had arrived at his office with a fresh head injury. The woman's husband had thrown an ax at her, slicing her head open. Her daughter closed the wound with a needle and thread. The woman needed an attorney because of a landlord–tenant dispute. Domestic violence was not an issue. This was before Lenore Walker.

Friday nights out were always difficult for us. We both needed to recover from our emotionally draining work. I had a history of falling asleep early on Friday night—sleeping through many great movies, like *If* and *Dr. Zhivago*. But I remember vividly the first Shabbat evening on the west side.

Smells from the kitchen instantly attacked nostrils, as we passed through the doorway. Decor was 1940. Definitely a walk back in time. Immediately, the feeling was "other world"—like my Aunt Sarah's apartment in Chicago on Shakespeare Avenue.

The white lace tablecloth, the silver candlesticks, the best china. The long table with so many places set. Dark walls and dim light. The feeling of specialness throughout the house. Immediately.

Excited children (so many) yelling, *"ema, ema" (mother, mother).* It was like a party. The experience bathed in a glow, like the first time I saw my husband's mother light the Sabbath candles.

It took my breath away.

Those west-side Orthodox families who invited us into their homes were genuine. No talk of clothes or trips or hairdressers. No questions about what sorority I pledged when I was in college. The women were articulate and bright. Extremely dynamic. I was impressed with their solidness. And I felt good around them. Incredibly welcome and comfortable.

> But
> the men/women stuff
> the separation
> bothered me.

Orthodox men and women don't sit next to each other during services. There is a *mekhitza,* a barrier, separating them. I knew that. But this was dinner.

A banquet-like table, with so many places set, filled the space of the large dining room. Men sat on one side, women on the other. At this very wide table, we couldn't get much farther apart.

After dinner we were all in the kitchen. I should say, all the women were in the kitchen. The men sat unmoved at the table, discussing the Torah portion for the week.

My uninvited eyes peeked through the kitchen doorway at what seemed to be a unique moment in time. No idle after-dinner conversation here. One of the men would say a word or two, everyone would take a deep breath, then nothing.

They seemed to be listening to each other's thoughts and appeared connected by both breath and silence. One moment loud voices, the next complete stillness. An intense contrast.

I know this sounds strange, but the room—the walls— seemed to be breathing in and out, along with the men. Just one continuous breath. Everything was connected.

> My eyes fixed
> on their
> passion
> and
> time stopped
> for me.

These men, intensely involved, not in talk of politics, but in a passionate philosophical discussion about one specific line in the Torah.

All night long.

It was luscious to watch as I did from the other side of the room. Visions of the past. Excluded. I felt childlike. A little kid who had snuck downstairs to listen to the grown-ups talk after dinner. I could only observe.

I thought it peculiar that none of the women approached the men or entered the Torah discussion. Were they not allowed? Was this another piece of Orthodoxy I did not understand? I wanted to do more than watch and listen.

>With no sound
>I shouted to myself.
>*I had something*
>*to say.*
>But
>to the men
>at the long table
>I was
>invisible.

Warmth and comfort filled the kitchen, yet I ached to be part of the magic in the other room.

Those remarkable Shabbat evenings, reminiscent of the sixties, were so attractive, even seductive, to us. There was a feeling of intimacy rarely experienced elsewhere. We both knew something very special existed in those strictly observant homes.

Despite our discomfort with many of the laws of observance, we considered jumping feet first into that remote existence. Our sojourns to the west side were extremely comforting, as those observant families seemed to offer something that was lacking in our life. But I remained concerned with the separation and the way some of the men related to the women.

It was lonely in this town of ours. Our families were far away, and Denver sometimes felt so isolated. Even though we made good friends, we didn't always have the emotional connections we needed. I believe we recognized our dissatisfaction not as a longing for spirituality but as a quest for a deeper relationship with people.

We struggled with the Orthodox laws that felt so strange and appeared archaic—laws so removed from our daily existence. The ritual felt good and served a definite purpose, but a move to Orthodoxy created barriers to our social interactions and our circle of close friends.

We suddenly realized that if we observed *kashrut*, the Jewish dietary laws, we would not have one non-Orthodox friend who could have us over for dinner. Ever again. That meant distancing ourselves from the good friends we had come to love.

I know—for a brief moment—we thought observant life was possible for us. But a move to an ultra-Orthodox life represented a radical change in every facet of our existence. We did not seem able to make the leap, even though our spiritual appetites had been fueled.

At this point in time, Judaism seemed to offer us three distinct paths of observance—Orthodox, Conservative or Reform.

The Orthodox path created impediments to our current existence. The Conservative had ritual and Hebrew in services and didn't separate men and women, but it lacked the intensity and intimacy of the Orthodox. The Reform stripped its members of any outward manifestation of ritual and seemed almost uncomfortable with being Jewish.

Reform services felt empty and void of spirituality.

I encountered people at all levels of observance who appeared disinterested. Many talked and laughed throughout services, anxiously waiting for them to be over. Or they arrived very late and were disruptive when they found their seats. The experience of attending services was not positive, and it created a definite dilemma. We struggled with spiritual questions and came to believe that answers would never be found within a Jewish framework.

We were not the first to distance ourselves from Jewish observance because we felt we had no place for a meaningful experience. During the sixties many Jewish seekers were attracted to other religions. In *The Jew in the Lotus*, author Rodger Kamenetz referred to "curious Jews exploring Buddhist teaching and leaving Judaism altogether." For a long time Boulder probably had many Jews who were more comfortable chanting a Buddhist mantra than a Hebrew prayer.

A piece was still missing as we sometimes experienced emptiness in our lives. Our quest was for increased consciousness, a deeper spiritual existence and the ability to quiet the mind. We were *on the path* —to where, I do not believe we knew.

I was pregnant when we were invited to the first night of Yom Kippur services at a neighborhood Reform synagogue. My husband and I had not been inside a Jewish house of worship since we had signed our *ketubah* (marriage contract) and recited our sacred vows of marriage. More than ten years earlier.

A special friend of ours accompanied the Kol Nidrei service with his cello. I had never heard the service with cello accompaniment before, and it was haunting. I recall being taken to another place by the Aramaic chanting and the visceral sound of the music. The feeling was intense. I sat motionless, with closed eyes and fixed hands that rested on the growing miracle inside me.

This was a time to go within, an early attempt to understand self—to inventory our life and closely examine what was not working. This was a first hint of self-awareness and an introduction to moral inventory.

We worked the Twelve Steps, dabbled in Eastern religion, began to meditate and practiced yoga. I had a

frightening experience with *Om Mani Padme Hum* and
came to understand why doing this work without a spiritual teacher was risky. Our bookshelves were filled with
Ouspensky, Gurdjieff, Castaneda, Buber, Swami
Muktenanda, Heschel and Ram Dass.

We ate mung beans and rice at Hannuman's Cafe and
talked of the here and now. I bought my first book on
Kabbalah (Jewish mysticism) and attended sessions in
Boulder with Trungpa Rinpoche (a Tibetan Buddhist). I
thought *Cutting Through Spiritual Materialism* was the
greatest book I had ever read. Our lives did not exactly have
direction.

When our daughter was three we were invited to a
havurah, a small, alternative religious group. It had been
formed recently and was close to our home. About ten
families came together to study Jewish texts, celebrate the
holidays and observe Friday evening Shabbat services.
There was no rabbi, no synagogue, and the men and
women sat together, as a family.

Services were held in a member's home and led by a
wonderful man from Boulder with rabbinic lineage and

training. Some prayers were read in English, but much
of the service was chanted beautifully in Hebrew.
Immediately one knew that this was a very different Jewish
experience.

A feeling of intimacy and genuineness pervaded. No one
flipped and counted pages in anxious anticipation of when
the service would finally be over. No one talked during the
service. People seemed happy to be present as they prayed
and sang with incredible enthusiasm. It was a profound
sensation. The only way to explain it is to say that I *felt* the
Shabbat service—inside my body. This was the first time I
had experienced spirituality during a Jewish service. I had
not thought it possible.

By accident, or so we thought, we found a religious
group that offered much of what we were attracted to on
the west side. We were instantly welcomed with warmth
and authenticity. After many years of drifting spiritually,
without any past Jewish commitment, we made a leap. We
joined the *havurah*.

With its unique form of observance, this group satisfied
a deep spiritual hunger that I believe surprised both of us.
It was a wonderful gathering of special families. Our
involvement intensified as our religious observance
increased. Friday was no longer our movie night.

The *havurah* expanded to the size of a small congrega-tion. Many of our members, who at first knew no Hebrew, were now reading from the Torah and leading services. We had religious celebrations for our children as they grew in knowledge and age. Our families celebrated, studied and prayed together with *kavenah* (intention).

There was a special glow at *Bellaire* on Friday nights.

As a family we had our own banquet-like Shabbat din-ners, with china and sterling and great smells as you walked through the turquoise-blue door. Friends talked of the magic in our house on Shabbat.

> I lit the Sabbath
> candles
> as
> we honored the setting
> sun.

The *havurah* was to nourish our souls, intellectually and spiritually, for a long time. Until my husband wanted more.

4

An Orthodox Life

few years before our daughter's *bat mitzvah* (a girl's
transition into responsible Jewish adulthood), the
charismatic Hasidic rabbi from the west-side community moved his entire congregation to the east side—our
side of town. This huge undertaking meant that his special
Orthodox services were now walking distance from our house.

My husband had begun to attend services, occasionally,
at Reb Moshe's new east-side *shul* (house of worship). But
during the year of our daughter's *bat mitzvah*, he committed
to full membership in the Orthodox group, attending
weekly Shabbat services with the rabbi.

I don't think I realized at the time how significant this was. Even though I now found myself at our *havurah's* weekly Shabbat services sitting next to my daughter, with her father noticeably absent. It was hard to explain to members that during this year of family commitment to our daughter's religious coming-of-age we were not in observance as a family. Talk about sleepwalking.

In Reb Moshe's Orthodox synagogue, a *mekhitza* partitions the men's and women's sections, with a high fencelike barrier. There are no *bat mitzvahs,* as women are not allowed to touch or read from the Torah or to lead services. Despite the prohibitions against women's participation, my husband's experience was good. The members of the *shul* were so hospitable and gracious to him—like many years ago.

He began to meet new people and had wonderful Shabbat experiences. It was understandable that he wanted to share this with his daughter. He asked her to attend services with him on Shabbat, but she was reluctant. She had been to services before at Moshe's *shul* and was disappointed by the experience.

"If I go with Dad," she said to me, "we can't even sit

together. I really like Rabbi Moshe and all the people there, but it's noisy on the women's side. I can't even see the Torah from behind the *mekhitza*."

This was my daughter's year of absorption in Hebrew study and ritual observance. After many years of preparation for her *bat mitzvah,* she was now learning to chant from the Torah and read the sacred script. In addition, she enthusiastically took on increased responsibility as she learned to chant most of the Hebrew service while studying an additional reading, a *haftorah.*

Intensified seventh-grade academics made this an increasingly difficult year for my daughter. Whether it was Mr. Hickey's mythology class or Madame Guiberteau's French instruction, academics at Graland were fairly intense. And without realizing it (when we chose the date) the *bat mitzvah* had been scheduled for the week after her final exams.

I do not know how she did it all, but she did, even as her parents continued along divergent spiritual paths. She grew up with the *havurah.* This was not the time for dividing her spiritual loyalty. This could have been a year of coming together as a family. It should have been. It was not.

My husband continued his progression toward a more religious life, as we both increased our observance. After he

left our home permanently, he became even more observant, choosing to live the insular existence of the ultra-
Orthodox. I understood if it gave him peace.

The community called him *ba'al teshuva* (one who
returns to Orthodoxy). He stopped driving, conducting any
business or talking on the telephone on Shabbat. He
strictly observed the laws of *kashrut,* which included no
pork, no shellfish, no mixing of milk and meat.

Keeping the laws of *kashrut* was not as simple as avoiding beef stroganoff or pepperoni pizza. For example, if you
had steak for dinner, you could have no ranch dressing on
the salad, no sour cream on the potato, no butter on the
rolls, no ice cream for dessert. It's much more complicated
than just staying away from lobster or steak with béarnaise
sauce. You have to watch the clock too, as time is involved.

My daughter told me that her father was making his new
kitchen *kosher* in strict adherence to the dietary laws. This
meant separate dishes for dairy meals and meat meals. A
dish could not be used for a cheese sandwich one day and a
turkey sandwich the next. This was quite a distance from
the green chili at Señor Miguel in Boulder.

❧ ❧ ❧

I could not help but recall how much of our history together revolved around great restaurant memories. As college students there were late-evening double cheeseburgers, brownie sundaes and chocolate malts at King's in Boulder. And Kroll's in Green Bay, where the cheeseburgers seemed to float on the greasy waxed paper.

There was a special birthday celebration at the Gondolier, when we secretly poured wine into the creamers. The restaurant was close to Boulder High, and Gary and Warren were not allowed to sell liquor. And Frank always made us feel so special at the Gold Hill Inn.

I know my husband will never forget our first Thai experience in Boulder, with Paula and Richard—who is no more. One of those nights when we smoked a little too much before dinner. Every tiny course came out s-l-o-w-l-y, and we attacked each appetizer plate before it touched the tablecloth.

I thought about our first Thanksgiving dinner at the Normandy, and those $2 dinners at the Lotus Room in the VFW hall. The incredible noodle soup at Little Pepina's, and M & G's with the best and hottest green chili. Our weekly trips to La Neueva Poblana and the wonderful sopapillas. Nothing beat the taste of a mesquite-broiled scallops dinner at the Fresh Fish Company. Or lobsters, courtesy of Pixie's lab.

A life together
seen through the
eyes
of a restaurant
menu.

Food and eating out were an important part of our history and a constant source of joy for my husband. His level of observance now meant there were only two restaurants in Denver where he could eat—the Mediterranean Cafe and the East Side Kosher Deli. He would never taste the New York steak at Brook's or the crème brûlée at the Barolo Grill. That was a very sad thought.

My husband advanced rapidly toward another existence, a different time and place. Something that resembled the Amish more than Jewish families in southeast Denver. He made the leap.

5

Get Fears

Once every week, for approximately twenty-six hours, a holy day is observed. Each week from just before sundown on Friday to just after sundown on Saturday, observant Jews follow extremely specific rules, regulations and prohibitions. For example, during this inclusive period, no work is allowed, no making of fires, no tearing of toilet paper. It is the Sabbath—the Jewish day of rest.

No driving or riding in cars, trains or planes. No snowboarding at Copper Mountain, visits to Coors Field, listening to CDs, going to the movies or watching TV. No

Saturday morning cartoons. No one is allowed to touch money, talk on the telephone or write.

No Saturday business on the golf course. No football games or trips to the mall. No Friday night dances or teenagers on the telephone.

No Internet communication or computer games. No e-mails, faxes or voice-mail messages. No studying for the big calculus exam or writing that letter to a friend.

Think about it. High school football games are usually played on Friday nights. The Kentucky Derby is always on a Saturday afternoon. Kids' lacrosse and soccer games are scheduled for Saturday mornings. The opening ceremonies of the Olympics are on Friday night, and NFL championship games are sometimes played on Saturday afternoons. The other world is oblivious.

> When you keep Shabbat
> it defines every aspect of
> your life
> and
> it is
> forever.

In observing the Sabbath, there is little argument about

whether something is allowed or not. The prohibitions are in writing. There is a manual to follow: the Torah.

Many years ago, at my annual women's retreat, I asked a good friend how she was able to keep Shabbat every week.

"How are you able to do it all in the midst of your hectic, high-profile professional life?" I asked.

She looked at me with an odd expression and said, "I could not do what I do without the Sabbath."

Shabbat is special time. Time regulated by the sun, not a clock. A period of contemplation, prayer and quieting of the mind. A time in which to honor our souls. A special island in time. It separates us from the rest of the week. It protects us from the rest of the week. It is a time to go within. It is *holy time*. It is a gift.

Over time I began to see how strict religious observance could simplify and enrich life. Part of me was actually a bit envious of my husband's spiritual commitment.

Many of the Orthodox families I knew had very special homes, with no feeling of sacrifice. It felt more like abundance. My husband moved toward a beautiful world. For a man, it made perfect sense.

He found comfort in his new life and acceptance by the
Orthodox community. He spent his time immersed in reli-
gious study, and he became more knowledgeable about
Jewish ritual and law. I believed he knew more about this
Jewish divorce than I did.

Just thinking about the *get* prompted visions of dark
cluttered rooms and *The Chosen*. The concept was uncomfortably distant from my reality. Extremely foreign. I didn't
even know anyone who had gone through the process. I
thought that was odd. And I found no one who greeted me
with "Let me tell you what a wonderful experience the *get*
was." To be honest, if my husband had not encouraged it, I
probably never would have thought about it myself.

His calls came often. He said that he wasn't asking
much. He just wanted my sanction. The *get* was actually his
to give to me but, as he explained, I had to be in full agreement. Even more important, there could be no coercion. I
had to agree to accept the *get* under my own free will. In
order to complete the Jewish divorce, most importantly,
mutual giving and receiving were necessary.

It seemed easy enough. All I had to do was talk on the

telephone to a rabbi and answer a few questions. Simple. They could do the rest without me. My presence during the process was not even necessary. All I had to say was "I grant you this Jewish ending."

But I was reluctant. I knew there had to be more involved than just answering a few questions and giving my okay. The *get* was both a ceremony and a document verifying the end. It had to be more than a simple process—more than a ritual—more than a piece of paper.

My husband was ready to have the *get* completed in the midst of our divorce mediation, but I continued to question the appropriateness of doing it before permanent orders were final. Didn't we need closure to our civil dissolution before we could have a ritual Jewish ending?

Final. End. Decree. Harsh words describing something illusive and positioned in the extremely distant future. Our settlement negotiations were not moving forward quickly. In three months of mediation we had agreed to one issue— how we would divide mediation costs. Nothing more.

My husband's attorney, who was simply looking out for the welfare of his client, appeared to be doing everything to continue the animosity. It seemed that whenever we approached agreement, negotiations would dissolve.

I did not understand my husband's comments about not having any money. "My practice is down," he would say. I wondered how his income could drop so drastically, so quickly. He was the senior partner in a highly successful law firm. Now his law clerks were making more money. It made me crazy to think that I could not trust him. Rod Serling had to be watching.

> The level of trust
> we once
> shared
> had slowly
> eroded
> and
> disappeared.
>
> It felt like a wound in the universe
> and
> it made me very sad.

6

Reb Kalman

Kalman Yoseph—a charismatic Hasidic rabbi—is equally comfortable in dialog with the Pope and the Dalai Lama. When he speaks, you feel his words.

His brilliance exists on more than one plane.

Reb Kalman—large, tall, powerful—inside and out. There is healing in his face. You can feel his presence from across the room. There is just no one like him. Anywhere.

> The most wonderful smile.
> And those special knowing eyes.

This uniquely gifted rabbi exposed me to a richness and depth in Judaism—knowledge previously foreign to me. Until my first Kalman retreat, Alan Watts and Carlos Castaneda rested on my nightstand—not Martin Buber or Abraham Heschel.

As a little kid I felt more comfortable with Christianity. Religion was not part of my childhood experience. When I began school in Chicago, I returned home one day and asked my mother, "What's a dirty Jew?" An angry little girl had called me a name at recess. I did not understand the meaning of her accusations.

My parents understood no Hebrew but spoke Yiddish, a German dialect written with Hebrew characters. During the winter holiday season we had a tree and not a menorah. My mother, orphaned at a young age, was comforted as a child by Catholic nuns. As an adult she found spiritual strength in attending Christmas eve Mass at Holy Name Cathedral.

In summer camp I attended Protestant, not Jewish, services. The prayers were in English and easy to follow. "The Lord is my shepherd" made sense but "Shema Yisrael" made me uncomfortable.

The Jewish services were unfamiliar, with strange songs and words. I felt out of place. Pretty much like an outsider. But I also felt ashamed. I could not read one Hebrew word in the prayer book.

> It's second grade and
> I'm the only kid in the room
> who can't read.

Synagogue, where everyone else seemed to know what to do, never felt welcoming. I was always on the wrong page. Too ashamed to ask, I sat forever confused and alienated.

No one seemed interested in the services. People talked about politics and clothes, and you had to pay for tickets to attend. Important members were able to sit up close to the Torah; less influential worshipers sat in the back. And when you were in the back, you could not hear beyond the din of the constant conversation around you.

The prayers were repeated very quickly, in a rote manner, without much thought or feeling. People counted pages to see how much more they had to endure.

Jewish spirituality.
I thought it was
an
oxymoron.
Until the *havurah*
and
Reb Kalman.

It is interesting that I never viewed the west-side Orthodox Shabbat experiences as spiritual. Those special nights touched me deeply without much understanding. I knew they felt good, but I did not understand why.

After my first *havdalah* (ceremony celebrating the end of Shabbat) service, I threw my arms around Kalman and cried. He looked me in the eyes with that great smile and said, "Welcome home."

I was hooked.

Kalman had known us for years. When my daughter was five, our family was at a Shabbat retreat together. Something caused her to be sad and Kalman made her smile. She wrapped her arms around his legs and asked him

if he would be her grandfather. He took a ring from his finger and placed it on hers.

> *This too shall pass*
> was the Hebrew inscription
> on the ring.

Reb Kalman Yoseph was in town conducting a two-day
workshop at a neighborhood synagogue. I offered him a
place to stay for the evening. My wonderful house was close
and comfortable and it would provide renewal from the
day's work. My daughter and I would be honored by his
presence in our home, even for one short evening.

I planned to let him have the entire upstairs of the
house—those three large, pleasant, sunny rooms where he
could regenerate and pray. The space would be good for his
morning *davening*, his morning prayers.

I had no intention of spending any time with him. Just
knowing he was upstairs would be a gift. I simply wanted to
provide the vehicle for his respite. I knew that his presence
was in demand and his time was precious. Spiritual leaders
were like that. They didn't have much unobstructed time.

Folks always wanted words of wisdom. Or healing. It was the same with Reb Moshe.

>   *Excuse me, Rabbi.*
>   *I just need five minutes.*

Kalman knew of my separation, but I had no intention of disturbing him with any details. He needed time to himself. Pretty selfless on my part, as I could have stayed up all night talking with him. Listening to his profound intellect and elegant prose would have lifted my spirits.

We drove home after the workshop. I showed him the rooms upstairs, he smiled, and I told him to have a good sleep. I knew he was tired.

As I began to walk downstairs I was taken by surprise when he stopped me and said, "I want to talk with you. I want to talk about the *get*."

Instantly I realized that allowing Kalman his personal space was not a selfless act on my part. I suddenly understood that I was actually afraid to talk with him. As his simple request resonated throughout my body, I felt his words in my chest. In this brief moment I became Marlow in anticipation of meeting Kurtz. The Zen of awe and fear. How did Kalman know?

Synchronicity. It was pretty much the same when I worked the Twelve Steps with Jack. In those days AA folks frowned on anyone who wasn't a drunk being involved in the program. But Jack took me on despite the prohibition. He would just call. "We need to meet," he would say. "You're not okay."

He knew my mental state before I did, and he was on the other side of town. Some gifted teachers just know things when there is no reason for their knowing. Someone else to whom I owe my life.

I stood frozen in time. Kalman was about to hand me a present and I had to be ready. "Listen carefully," I said to myself.

He took a deep breath as he continued slowly.

"The *get* is very special. But it can be a not-so-good

experience. I don't want you hurt by the process."

At this moment he nodded and tilted his head with that apprehensive yet comforting expression. We had direct eye contact and it was as though his words entered my consciousness through the connection of our eyes. Hard to explain, but this was not verbal communication.

Kalman continued.

"A *get* can be overwhelming, intimidating and even humiliating for women. Very painful. But it can also be an incredibly powerful healing experience. It will help you to be truly separate."

Another deep breath. He paused again, making sure we experienced direct eye contact. That was his way.

> *I want it to be good for you.*
> *I want you protected.*

I was not ready to respond. Uncomfortable and unpre-pared—wishing I had thought this out ahead of time. I had so many questions. I wanted to make the best use of this special moment. *But I also did not want to drain him, and I am carrying on all these simultaneous conversations in my head before I develop any idea of what I will say.* There was so much

going on—it was so *noisy* in there that I was amazed when
I was able to respond with a sense of normalcy.

> It really didn't
> matter
> because Kalman knew
> all that
> anyway.

I began to talk about the conflict over when to do the *get*.
It was a difficult conversation as I tried not to say anything
hurtful about my husband. It was hard not to let the negative spill out, but I knew that would be wrong. I was aware
of the prohibition in Jewish law of *lashon harah* (damaging,
hurtful speech), and I also knew Kalman cared for my husband. In the reality of the moment, none of this had any
meaning. Kalman would never allow me to say anything
unkind about my husband, at least not in his presence.

> I walked the tightrope
> above
> the ground
> but had
> difficulty with

the
footwork.

I explained how we were in disagreement. I struggled for
noncritical words. I told Reb Kalman, "He wants to do the
get now and I want to wait." I said that I was not completely
sure why, but that I felt strongly about waiting to do the *get*
until our civil divorce was final.

Reb Kalman agreed about waiting.

He said that I needed to understand how important it
was to take the time necessary to learn about the process.
He suggested that I ask Reb Moshe to be present during
the actual writing of the *get*. Kalman looked gently at me as
he said, "Moshe is honored and revered. If he is there, they
will be good to you."

He was talking about
the *black hats*.

I explained to Kalman that Rabbi Moshe had already
offered to teach me about the process. In addition, Moshe
said he would be present during the *get* if I wanted him
there. I told Kalman that I felt incredibly thankful just
knowing that Moshe would guide me through the process.

It helped greatly with my anxiety about the unknown and my fear of being the *other*.

Reb Kalman was quite solemn in the few short minutes that we were together. He seemed determined to impart to me that, above all, I needed to be—in his words—"conscious" and "aware" when I ended my marriage. This was not a time for sleepwalking.

"We have a ceremony to begin a life together. The *get* is the ceremony to end a life together. Approach the *get* with respect and awe. Use it wisely."

He smiled that wonderful smile and I knew it was time to say good night.

I was beginning to understand.

7

The Economics
of Divorce

We talked again about remaining friends during the settlement process. I liked that idea. He had been my friend first, before he was my lover. But our civil divorce negotiations had turned nasty. He didn't feel like a friend.

Suddenly, we were at war with each other over money. It was so strange. Money had been such a minor issue in our life together. But not anymore as I now feared for my economic survival.

It did not help to learn that even though he repeatedly

promised that college money for our daughter would never be an issue, now he was saying it was.

He painted a bleak economic picture of his finances, explaining that his highly successful law practice had been drastically reduced. And he filed papers with the court stating that his family trust was nonexistent. He wanted me to understand. "I'm all tapped out," he would say.

For me, this was like a shift in the universe. The feelings were so profound. It disturbed me to consider the possibility that he might be untruthful while explaining his financial situation. I was not prepared to question the veracity of his statements, especially considering his increased religious practice.

But people had warned me.

"Save the angry messages," they suggested. "You can use them in court."

I was shaken by the thought of stockpiling ammunition to use against my husband—even if there were a possibility of his untruthfulness.

After all . . .

He had always been the one.

He was the one with whom I shared my bed. The only man I had ever been intimate with.

The concept of deception was so unsettling. As I said before, it unbalanced me.

Several months passed. The realities of my economic situation frightened me, and many of my thoughts were not altruistic. Knowing that the *get* was something my husband wanted was enough reason to withhold it from him. I must say that idea entered my consciousness. But I knew I could never hold that ancient ritual hostage. It was never a possibility—never more than a hurtful momentary thought.

I wrestled with questions continually, talking to myself a lot. Trying not to let people notice. Only conversing when I was sure no one was around. My daughter became concerned when I visited her during her first Parents' Weekend at college.

"You're talking to strangers in the popcorn line at the movies. Mo-omm. You're stressed and you're spending too much time alone." She was right—as always.

I began to view the divorce in the context of grief. Seeing it that way made sense to me. After all, it felt physically like death. The losses seemed insurmountable.

> Just no body
> to bury.

One passed through definite phases of grief. Each week felt different from the week before. I needed time to get used to the idea of divorce. I still could not use the word in conversation.

Why did it seem so easy for him to move quickly, almost immediately, into another intense relationship? Didn't he know that the pain of our ending had to be worked through first in order to be truly separate? It made no sense that he was considering marriage before the emotional work was done. But he was.

Unkind thoughts sometimes won out as I struggled to make emotional sense of my life. I came to view my husband's anxiety over the *get* as his need for a guarantee. I believe he wanted insurance that he could marry again, as soon as our civil divorce became final.

Marriage, I thought.
I fought my father
for this man.
My passionate lover
and
partner for life.

Augie was not pleased. He liked the other boy. The quiet one. Augie was used to his way. After several years of college dating, it was *him* they expected as a son-in-law, many years down the road. Not this brash new kid who marched in and never even asked permission.

So angry
unprepared
and
not honored.
Where did this
new boy
come from?
He wondered.

"Why are you so anxious to get married?" my father asked. "You're so young. What's the rush?"

"I want to wake up with him next to me. Forever."

> Just two kids
> so consumed by
> love and
> passion.
> I loved him deeply.
>
> *Zits and all?* he used to ask.
> Yes, I would affirm.
>
> And with youthful arrogance
> we thought that
> no one could really understand
> the depth of our experience.

My heart raced. I needed more time to battle my own intellect. Vulnerability fueled self-doubt. Insecurity overwhelmed. Negative thoughts drenched my consciousness. I did not believe that my Orthodox husband truly understood our Jewish ending, or the extreme lifelong consequences of our divorce.

During one fairly awful period, as I watched our daughter being ripped in two, I left a voice-mail message pleading for a chance to talk about the destruction we were bringing about. He did not return my call. He probably never even thought about responding.

Whenever we spoke about anything, the conversation eventually turned to the *get*. My responses became repetitive and predictable—almost boring.

"The time is not good. Emotionally I need to be further along. The wounds are still fresh." He did not understand that I was not ready *psychologically*.

His persistence seemed almost comical. One day he just called to arrange the *get*. No more asking. No more "Is this date okay?" He must have thought, "I'll just set a date and she will be there."

He told me simply on the telephone, "The scribe will be in town in two days. He can write the *get* then. He won't be back for a few months. Let's just get it done with."

I said that I was not available in two days and repeated my concerns. I explained again that this difficult experience needed time. It seemed to be a good conversation—a comfortable exchange of words.

"I understand completely," he responded. "I agree with your concerns."

He sounded compassionate and accepting. I was pleased. But a minute or so passed and he followed those considerate words with a familiar request.

"The scribe will be in town next Tuesday. Could you do it then?"

My message was simply not getting through.

8

What Was I Missing?

If in the telling it seems repetitive—that's because it was. The requests continued, becoming almost a metaphor of the process itself. Calls now came from an Orthodox rabbi I did not know.

He called late at night, around 10:30. Not a good time. He identified himself quickly. "This is Rabbi ____." I never could understand his name.

Immediately he began to ask questions.

> very softly
> very quietly
> very intensely

"What is your name? What are you called? What is your father's name? Did he have any other names?"

I remember being flooded with fear after hearing the simple question, "Were there other names that your father was called?" Who was this stranger asking me about my father?

I became sad and frightened. I stopped eating and sleeping. I discovered those weird television shows at 3:00 A.M. for people who were part of the *sleepless* culture. Depressed, low-self-esteem folks who didn't have a job, an education, an income or a life. Tony Robbins and Fran Tarkenton on three channels simultaneously—telling us how to improve our lives. It was a dark world I knew nothing about.

My weight dropped significantly. I had always been thin. Now I was *scary* thin. I found no pleasure in food or the bed I slept in. I looked awful. Luckily, there was one consistent factor in my life (besides my daughter) that gave me purpose and kept me going—my work. When I entered my office and closed the three doors to the outside world, nothing else existed. I was focused completely on the here and now.

For some odd reason, after my husband left I was unable

to sleep underneath the sheets or covers. I slept on the extreme left edge of the bed, on top of the blankets, almost afraid to touch the other side—the side with the history.

It was always in the middle of the night that the stinging sad thoughts intruded into my being. Like how excited we were when we finished the upstairs addition to *Bellaire* and shopped together for a new bed—our first queen size. It was such a special purchase. And oh how he loved the beautiful wood.

> I thought to myself.
> Forty-nine, single and alone.
> My mother didn't plan this.

I did not like what I had become, as I seemed consumed with sadness and confusion. I feared losing all the important people in my life. I thought for sure that my best friend would tire of listening to me. My sister was great and always listened, but we lived a thousand miles apart.

The confused emotions I experienced daily were difficult to articulate. Words were not adequate. The harsh reality was that people comfortable within their marriages who had never experienced the depths of divorce just did not understand.

There were feelings I did not understand and could not

explain—thoughts about which I was ashamed. Fears that had no rationale. Only members of the club could decipher the code. There was even a secret handshake for those who never wanted to join.

My daughter and I remained close, but she was far away in Maine at Bowdoin College. Not exactly driving-home-for-the-weekend distance.

This was her first year of college and the beginning of a new life. She had her own struggles. It was not right for me to call a not-yet-settled first-year college student, two thousand miles from home and say, "Hi, how are you? Your mom feels like shit." She did not need my pain. It would not help her with the complexities of organic chemistry.

But it was hard to give in to the good-mom side, as I self-ishly wanted my daughter to know how awful it was. In a reversal of roles, I needed her to make it all better and tell me that life would be improved some day. Because right now . . .

           it hurt so much
           and
           nothing
           made the ache less
           intense

that I wasn't so sure
about a
tomorrow.

How does one survive? I asked myself over and over. How does anyone make it through? Thoughts wandered to my husband. What was he doing to cope? Oh. Yes. She made the ache less intense. If there was an ache.

I was devastated when I lost both my mother and my father in one year, yet this pain permeated my essence in an even more profound way. With the divorce, my entire reality was being reordered—strangeness enveloped me. It wasn't just the loss of my husband; it was everything that defined my married existence. I told myself that it was time for emotional honesty. My reaction to the loss frightened me. I feared that I would never feel normal again. If I didn't confront my feelings now, then I knew,

I would
never be
free.

As the man in the TV commercial said, "Pay me now or pay me later." One does not really have a choice. The emotional work eventually has to be done, or we pay in some way.

> I needed to be alone, and to do the work now.
> That was not a pleasant thought.

Little girls never get a chance to be alone. They have mothers, boyfriends, roommates, husbands and then children. Even the word had a frightening sound. Detached. Isolated. Removed. Remote. Alone.

Unknowing people would say, "You've been separated for a year. Let go. Stop being sad. Just pull your life together. You're strong. Move on. It's just a divorce."

Their uninformed words did not help.

> If only they knew.
> The thought of death
> was so much more
> comforting.

I began to live month to month for the first time in my life. Suddenly, visits to the dentist became a luxury I could not afford. Such drastic changes, in less than a year. The list overwhelmed one's sense of normalcy.

My husband moved out, my kid left for college, my dog was sent away, my mountain house was gone, my home was sold, my financial stability was lost, friends were unavailable, family members became distant, my social life disappeared, and after thirty years of being faithful I became a threat to almost every married friend I had ever known.

Gone were Shabbat dinners, weekends at the mountain cabin, holiday celebrations, rituals, friends, dinners with couples, invitations, ski trips, scuba diving and—oh—island vacations. Would I ever see Little Cayman again?

Gone was the casual worry-free married existence that I took for granted for so many years. In an instant, I was no longer part of the Family. My husband's mother was now sending presents to the woman that would be her new daughter-in-law. I was off the holiday list, replaced so simply and quickly. Didn't she know how much I truly loved her?

I seemed to be losing all that had defined my life—my connections, supports, comforts, my identity. As my financial security disappeared, I asked myself, "Do I send my daughter a plane ticket to come home over spring break, or do I pay the tuition bill?" The father, who had made promises, did not exist anymore.

> How could this time and place
> be so far from
> the gift of the
> *Prophet*
> and
> the magic
> of our
> life together?

The sun had set and the glow was now gone. I would not have lost as much if my husband had just died. What an awful thought.

People did not know how insidious their avoidance was. Friends didn't want to choose one partner over the other, so many just avoided us both. When one of us was invited, it was usually my husband. It didn't matter that I was the one to drive the carpool, buy the birthday presents, take the kids to Chuck E. Cheese and plan the sleepovers. He was the one who got the invitations. Nothing prepared me for *dissolution's dirty little secret.*

It was so hurtful.

Friends became distant—those special people that I had been close to for twenty-five years—family without the umbilical cord. Our kids grew up together, from crib to college.

People joked that even our dogs had a close relationship. Mornings at Grand Lake, the dogs would scratch and paw at each other's cabin windows—kind of calling on each other. "Can Max come out and play?" they would ask with their barks and scratches.

While married, I experienced an active social life. Black-tie galas, dinner invitations, party invitations, just hanging out and going to the movies, or grabbing a quick bite to eat on a weeknight with another couple. We were always with friends. Now the invitations were nonexistent and the phone never rang. The silence had a life of its own, as these intimate friends, and others, simply vanished.

I hope I don't sound terribly bitter. I know I do. I was just so totally unprepared for the pain and the insensitivity. Had I done that to divorced friends during my comfortable married life? This was such a vulnerable time—a time when one's existence needed to be validated. It began to feel as though my previous life truly had been an illusion that had never existed.

I watched a reverse Polaroid of me as the image of my past life faded.

Without my husband (even though I was a professional with a business) I did not seem to exist socially. Whether it was a country club (not that I could afford one) or a *mikveh* (Jewish ritual bath), I was excluded because of my single status. This did not happen to men.

The Orthodox community had been very good to my husband after he moved from our home. He was openly accepted and sought out by members of the *shul*. Families fought over his presence at Shabbat dinner. I believe I was envious of his acceptance by this special community.

In contrast, much of my wonderful *havurah* appeared threatened by my new single existence and by the concept of divorce itself. I wanted to tell them that it was not contagious and that I had been faithful in my marriage. Instead of feeling accepted, I felt alienated.

For twenty years, folks in the *havurah* had been great at handling cancer, death, and even murder, but marital conflict seemed to terrify. Even eye contact was minimal. Some just could not look my way. People I loved—families with whom the ties had been strong—many never invited me to their homes again.

At this critical time in my life I needed the positive energy of others and some semblance of continuity from the past. But instead, people responded with fear and distance.

> That was
> *really*
> the most difficult
> loss
> of all.

If it were not for my incredible daughter, with understanding and words of wisdom. "The best is yet to come, Mom." If it were not for a few very good friends and family. If it were not for those special people who listened when they were so tired of listening. If it were not for the few *havurah* families, who loved me and made me part of their family—well, I do not know. I thank them for my life because

it was pretty bleak.

The rabbi with the unfamiliar name—well, I didn't like his late-night telephone calls. They upset me. I could not think clearly as the strangeness intensified—that floaty feeling of not being connected to anything. And the phone calls—they penetrated my sense of self.

There were many unknowns. Who was this person asking me questions? If I gave him information on the telephone was I giving the *get?* If I answered the questions, could the rabbinic panel complete the *get* without me?

When I expressed hesitation and reluctance to answer the rabbi's inquiries, he responded by saying to me, "You should just answer the simple questions. That is all I ask. I need this information—so I can begin to write the *get*."

My heart pounded in my ears. *You know you don't even have to be there. It really is not necessary. We can do this without you.*

His words echoed inside my head and caused a shudder as I realized

> he was beginning
> to write
> the *get*
> without me.

This was football without a game plan. Tiger Woods using borrowed clubs in the Masters. Nothing made any sense. Why all of the pressure and urgency if I didn't even have to be there? I was Alice spending the afternoon with the Queen.

> They just needed my okay.
> *No big deal,* I said to myself.

An orthodontist once told me that my oral surgery was going to be "a piece of cake," no big deal. He neglected to tell me that I would be in intensive care for two days and that there would be a tube down my throat so I could breathe. I had heard about things like that before. People do experience different realities.

If this Jewish ending was not very important, why the pressure? "No coercion," I recall my husband telling me. It had to be of "my own free will." What was I missing? It was crazy-making stuff. Every sensation alerted me that this ritual was something powerful, meaningful and significant. Why were the others treating it as though it were a simple Sunday morning run through Country Club?

It didn't take much perception on my part to realize that I was clearly not wanted at my own *get*. I finally understood that I truly was a minor player in this game. All they really needed from me was my consent. They cared nothing of the sacred ritual and its significance.

9

Sell the House?

Experiencing a divorce after many years of marriage is traumatic—but the word "trauma" is not sufficient to describe the experience. It just lies there on the page.

Trauma is a physical word.
It assaults one's essence.

"We're going to have to sell the house," he said casually. "Why don't you call a Realtor?"

Even though I knew we were going to have to sell the house, the words still resonated with a powerful impact.

I would never be ready to make that call.

Sell Bellaire? My head screamed without a sound. *What are we doing? This is crazy! We had so much together. Wait . . .*

With a desire to postpone the inevitable, I responded, "You're going to have to find a Realtor. I can't do it."

My husband never felt the same way I did about our house. Before we had separated, he wanted to sell our home and move closer to Reb Moshe's *shul.* His walk to services on Shabbat was difficult, especially in bad weather.

I don't think he saw *Bellaire* as the only home our daughter had ever really known.

The house where
all the

kids
hung out.

As though functioning on autopilot, they walked into the kitchen and pulled out the junk-food drawer. I think I kept it stocked just for them with potato chips, cookies and pretzels. Then they reached for a soda in the fridge.

How many kids could sit around that corner booth at once? I loved their sounds and the fact that they felt so comfortable. For hours. Talking, telling stories—always about guys and how oblivious they were, unless guys were present. The tears. And the giggles. I will miss the laughing and the noise.

This great house with huge old trees and a forest in the backyard.

> The squirrels
> that Osa chased
> the trees
> the light
> A very special place.

It was an accident—how we found out about the house. A convoluted set of circumstances guided by the stars. Our Realtor, who was also a good friend, was playing golf at the Cherry Hills Country Club, and he had a foursome with a man who was friends with a couple who was thinking about selling their home. There was no listing yet. No sign was up.

The market was hot in Hilltop, and it seemed like the only time real-estate signs went up was when they said "SOLD." And certain streets, certain blocks were highly desirable. Bellaire was one of those streets. Close to Cranmer Park and Graland.

"Why, I know the Moores," said our Realtor between golf shots. "I used to deliver papers to them when I was a kid. They live on Bellaire, don't they?"

That same day I went to look at the house. When we pulled up to the curb and I saw those giant trees, I told our Realtor that I didn't need to go inside. I knew. This was the final scene in *Miracle on 34th Street*. "Stop, stop. This is my house. The one I asked for. It is. It is. I know it is."

We moved in two months later.

It was a great move from the suburbs, where kids had to be driven everywhere. Our daughter could now walk to school. I remember sitting in front of the Perry & Butler SOLD sign, not quite believing that this incredible house, with the vines, was ours.

The first morning in our new home, while my husband and I slept, our little daughter rode her bicycle down to Aylard's Drug, sat down on one of the black swivel stools at the counter, ordered a chocolate ice cream soda and bought a greeting card.

When my husband and I woke that morning, we found a beautiful card placed in the center of the kitchen table. On the inside of the card she had so carefully printed "Dear Mom and Dad: Thank you for my wonderful new house."

In that special home, we celebrated birthdays, had slumber parties, carved pumpkins, baked chocolate chip cookies, lit Hanukkah menorahs, prepared Passover seders and kindled the Sabbath candles. Our neighbors were friends at barbecues and backyard picnics. We shoveled snow together, raked lots and lots of leaves and watched our children grow tall. I never thought of living anywhere else.

After we sold *Bellaire* and moved from our wonderful neighborhood, I received a note from one of my daughter's friends. He lived just a few houses away.

"I will miss you guys. I'll miss just knowing you're down the street."

"Me, too," I whispered to myself.

10

Transitional Objects

Moving from that house was rough. It had taken months just to get used to the thought. I still had trouble talking about it. Meetings with the Realtor were not happy get-togethers.

When the move was over and I had dealt with a lifetime of toys and memories, I was numb.

The move required two moving crews. One crew packed up my husband's things (which I marked with green

stickers), and the other crew packed my daughter's belongings and my things. To make the situation a bit more difficult, my daughter and I were moving to a temporary
residence. Boxes going there were marked with blue stickers. But most of our belongings were going to storage.
Those boxes were marked with red stickers.

The first crew arrived early in the morning, at about
8:00. These guys were great. I was convinced they all had
degrees in psychology. They understood when I began to
cry, as I explained the coding of the green, blue and red
stickers. This was not a joyous move.

This first crew was in charge of moving my husband's
things. They had to work quickly because it was Friday and
all of my husband's boxes needed to be inside his townhouse
before sunset and the beginning of the Sabbath. As I helped
pack up his belongings, I heard one of the guys shout from
down the hall, "Hey, where's your husband anyway? Why
isn't he here helping with the move?"

The morning went well. The movers were good at what
they did and fun to have around. It felt like having friends in
the house. I was going to be sad when their truck pulled away.

The move was going pretty well and I was somewhat upbeat—attempting to get my daughter to see that we were about to embark on an adventure. Those morning movers had a great way about them. They actually had us believing we were having fun.

The second crew had the job of moving boxes to our temporary residence and to the storage facility. This crew arrived before the first crew loaded all of my husband's belongings onto their truck. I showed the new crew around the house and explained the color coding to them—telling them that they were only responsible for moving my belongings.

As we stood together in my husband's study, I paused to talk to the lead mover of the second crew.

"You need to avoid the boxes with the green stickers," I said. "They go to my husband's townhouse. That stuff is being loaded on the truck now."

He looked at me and said, "No f---ing way. What's with all these f---ing stickers? I can't do this. It's too late in the day." He then began to throw boxes from one side of the room to the other.

At that moment, I didn't remember the joy in hanging the Hebrew mandala I bought as a present for my husband. Or notice how the light danced along the empty bookshelves in his study. I simply lost all emotional control. There was no thought before I began to scream. I do not recall what I shouted, but I am sure it was not nice. I ran outside to the head of the first moving crew and told him that I wanted that guy out of my house.

"If he can't show respect for my things and me, then I don't want him in my special home."

Soon there was a new lead mover for the second crew. I don't remember a great deal about him. He was not much of an improvement, but at least he didn't scream profanities.

It was about 3:00 in the afternoon when the house was emptied of our history together. As the trucks pulled away, my daughter and I realized that not only had we not rested once during the day—we hadn't eaten anything either.

We drove the few short blocks to the Cherry Creek Mall and ate at one of those California-type theme restaurants. It was not one of our better meals. Bad service and bad food best describe the experience.

As I recall there was not much conversation. Drained of emotion, we sat quietly—taking small bites of food. Neither of us was anxious to leave the restaurant. We had no enthusiasm for what awaited us at the end of our lunch.

We had executed the move from our home. In a few short, difficult hours, *Bellaire* had become a shell with no life force. The truck would now meet us at our new residence—a tiny one-bedroom apartment that lacked definition. Our venture from richness and depth to obscurity and uncertainty was now complete.

"Mom, what if we don't get the loan?"
"We'll worry about that if it happens."

While picking at our food we looked at each other and thought how luscious sleep would be. Exhaustion was too mild a word. "Can we stay longer?" my daughter asked, as our table was cleared of half-eaten sandwiches and diet sodas.

"I think we have to go. It's almost 5:00."

I handed the waiter my credit card and then signed the check. Reaching for my car keys, next to my daughter's sunglasses, seemed to make the inevitable real. But the thinking continued to be

> this is not me
> this is *not* happening to me.

As we walked from the restaurant into the mall, my daughter shouted, "My Oakleys, I left them on the table." She sprinted back inside. A minute later she came out.

"They're gone and the cleanup guy said there were no sunglasses in our booth. He said he would have seen them if they were there."

I went over to the manager and explained the situation, telling him that they were costly sunglasses and had only been left on the table for a matter of seconds. He told me that he would keep his eye out for them.

"What's your telephone number in case they turn up?"

"But they were just there," I said.

"I can't help you any more. No one saw any sunglasses."

It turned into a very expensive lunch.

When you're in a bad place, you become vulnerable. It's all about energy.

At the new apartment we tried to make the best of an unhappy situation.

"Let's hook up the TV and stereo," suggested my daughter. "Maybe one of these guys can help?"

One of the movers played around with some of the wires and said that everything was okay. We should have turned on the TV to see if it was working before I wrote the check, but we didn't. As it turned out nothing was connected correctly.

It was late and these guys were pretty anxious to leave us. At the end of a workweek, this unenthused crew didn't exactly seem to care if we were satisfied customers. It was 10:00 at night before the last box had been stacked inside. Not exactly a way to observe Shabbat.

Surrounded floor to ceiling by cartons piled everywhere, yet accompanied by a distinct feeling of isolation. We might as well have been at the South Col of Everest.

My daughter, feeling the fear of the loneliness, called a good guy friend to come over to help us set up the TV and stereo. I will never forget the look on her face when she opened the door and saw her friend's familiar smile. I know she had tears in her eyes as she threw her arms around his neck and grabbed tightly. It was almost a hold of desperation as they stood in the doorway and silently rocked back and forth.

We ordered pizza and laughed about the mess and old times. Like when he was twelve and smashed his head through one of her bedroom windows at *Bellaire*. Or when she nearly totaled his Honda, two days after getting her driver's license.

This great kid will never know that he was the one who got us through that first frightening night—as he came to define the meaning of friend. He became the transitional object as he helped us move beyond the intensity of emptiness and loss. *Bellaire* was gone. It was real now.

11

The Dingy
and the Prophetic

A few days later I found myself in the corporate offices of the moving company. There was some discrepancy in the bill. As I waited for the figures to be checked, I began to reflect on the move.

I explained to the clerk that the company's workers simply needed to be more sensitive—many folks were forced to let go of special places. "Some moves are just real hurtful experiences," I said.

I was emotionally battered and drained from the move, trying to convey this public-relations message to a strange woman who really didn't care about me, in the middle of an obscure moving company office. You know, musty odor, kind of gray walls, metal desks, papers everywhere, a vending machine off to one side, filled with nut clusters and chocolate bars, and windows that haven't been washed in a long time.

I remember saying something without much thought, like "Divorce is just so painful." Sort of a throwaway comment. I didn't know if she heard, and I wasn't even sure that I was talking to her.

She heard what I said and looked up at me from her desk. "I know," she responded.

This person who was unknown to me a few moments before began to talk candidly about her divorce and what she felt like during the ending of her marriage.

I remember feeling uncomfortable with her openness and apparent intimacy, as I jumped in and nervously told her about me. That I was feeling unbalanced, kind of like the way I felt after my parents died, only worse.

"Death would be easier," I suggested uncomfortably.

I felt ashamed when I realized I was more interested in telling her my story than listening to hers. You know when someone tells you something and then you stop listening to what they are saying because you are thinking about what you are going to say back to them?

I also wasn't so sure I wanted to know about her experience—her pain. But she continued anyway, unaware of my rudeness, as though she were talking to herself. It didn't seem to matter whether I was there or not. She didn't look at me, just stared off, like she was in a momentary trance.

"I kept a journal," she said. "I think it saved my life. The writing got me through it."

As she spoke she appeared to struggle to find the right words. I had a strong sense that this was something she had not thought of or talked about for a long time. She seemed to need to explain to me how she felt after thirty-five years of marriage.

"He just left one day," she said to me. "And I felt like—well, you know—when they hang those deer—and cut them open—and then their guts just fall out. Well, that was me. I was just hanging there. With my guts spilling out."

Her words stopped my breath, with an image I was *never* to forget. She put those difficult emotions into words, in a way that sliced me open. She nailed it down. At that penetrating moment, I felt and understood her experience.

> Deer hanging
> gutted
> after the kill

insides
streaming out
from the
gash
in the middle.

So I'm just hanging there, extremely vulnerable, not much solidness, and this strange person is calling me late at night asking me personal questions, and I'm not at my very best.

I was intimidated by the rabbi's calls and questions. I wanted to stop them but felt compelled to listen. Like when the phone rings at night and I hear a computer-generated call but continue listening, even when I know no human is on the other end. Sometimes it's hard to put the phone down. During one political election I got a call from Hillary Clinton. I felt guilty when I hung up without listening to everything she had to say.

I moved past the guilty, uncomfortable feelings and finally told the rabbi that I didn't want to talk to him. I told

him that I was not sure when I was going to do the *get* and
that I did not want him to call me anymore. It was a very
difficult conversation. He stopped calling afterward, but my
husband began to call—again.

I know as you're reading along you're thinking, "This all
seems pretty tedious. Not more calls. *Let's get it done.*" Well,
there is no shortcut in the telling or the experiencing.
Enduringly painful, wearisome. Essence of *Clockwork
Orange.* We are watching Alex view the horrific scenes on
the movie screen, with eyes wide open.

This experience is reminiscent of the nine-and-a-half-
hour Holocaust film *Shoah.* Director Claude Lanzmann
asks the survivors questions in French, which are asked
again in Polish by the translator with the Polish response
then translated back into French only to appear—many
seconds later—on the screen as English subtitles. The
process is slow and filled with silence allowing the significance of the shocking words to sink in. There is a purpose
to his method. Like Kubrick's work, it is frightening,
monotonous and brilliant.

Slow and boring and intense.
It is like going through the *get*
before the *get*.

Wasn't the *get* supposed to be a real separation, an end-ing, a break with the past, an actual severing of the ties of marriage? How could we go through this cutting and rip-ping and *then* proceed with our divorce negotiations?

My resolve strengthened, as did my clarity of purpose. The *get* could be therapeutic and healing. It could provide closure to our unending emotional bond. I thought to myself, "Timing is everything—one needs to pay attention to the order of things." Why didn't my husband know that? He was the religious scholar.

His comments continued and never varied.

"It's no big deal. Why wait? It takes just a few minutes. You don't even have to be there."

The calls still made no sense. Finally, I took a deep breath and just said, "I don't think we should do the *get* until we compete the civil divorce."

I tried to prepare for my husband's response, knowing that he would not be pleased.

"What do you mean wait until the divorce is final? I knew it. I knew this was what you were going to do. I *knew*

you were going to do this—use the *get* for economic pur-
poses. I knew you were going to hold it over me."

Soon those exact words were being whispered in the
Orthodox community. Rumor spread that I was using the
get as an economic tool so that I could obtain the best financial results in the divorce settlement.

This was an additional wound, to find out that others
were participating in *lashon harah,* the spreading of gossip.
In the eyes of God, this was an extremely serious offense.

12

Reb Moshe

It has been my fortune over the years to have experienced relationships with many gifted spiritual teachers. One special relationship was with Rabbi Avraham Moshe, the Hasidic leader of my husband's *shul*.

Even though I am not Orthodox, Reb Moshe has always been very accepting of me and nonjudgmental. I know he would like me to be more observant, but he never makes me feel bad that I am not. He simply accepts me. He knows my relationship with God is genuine.

With his long black coat and wonderful fur *Yom Tov* (holiday) hat, his long, graying beard, and his huge physical presence—there is no mistaking him for anything but a Hasidic leader.

His eyes charm, his smile soothes, his answers come slowly with a pointed heaviness. Every word counts. Nothing is wasted in conversation with Reb Moshe.

The pauses have power.

He is an Orthodox male dressed in black, but I always feel good about myself when we are together. He is never arrogant or condescending.

He has the greatest eyes.
Even though they see through you.

From time to time we would meet at his *shul*, where he dragged me through the emotional fragments of my dissolving marriage. We never talked about the *get*, even though he made several offers to help me understand the procedure. It was as though I feared him even mentioning the word.

Occasionally he approached the subject, but when he did my thoughts would wander, which was so odd because I was always extremely attentive in his presence. I generally savored every word from the rabbi.

I know now I was simply not ready to hear his words. The experience reminded me of a therapy session where the therapist suggests a painful piece of information. Sometimes instead of absorbing what could be a powerful insight into self, the patient falls asleep while the therapist is talking. Our defenses protect us from what we are not able to tolerate. When the time is right, the information becomes part of our consciousness. For some people the time is never right.

My husband's accusations that I was doing something wrong made me realize that I needed accurate information now. I had to be honest with myself about the *get*. The Scarlett O'Hara mentality was not appropriate. Avoidance thinking was just not working.

I called Reb Moshe and asked him if we could meet. I told him I was ready to hear what he had to say—that I had some specific questions I really needed answered. *Was I doing something wrong?*

Moshe suggested a meeting at his *shul*, with my husband present, explaining that it would be good for us to meet together and absorb, at the same time, specific information about the *get*. The two of us listening to the rabbi made good sense.

I had to say I was surprised by my husband's absence at the meeting, since our getting together with the rabbi meant that we were that much closer to something very important to him. It would have been good for both of us to hear what the rabbi was saying. My husband should have known that.

I needed to know if Reb Moshe thought I was wrong in wanting to wait until the civil divorce was final. So when we met, my first question to the rabbi had to do with timing. I simply asked, "When should we do the *get*? At what time in the divorce process is the *get* appropriate?"

Reb Moshe explained to me that ideally all divorce proceedings should be completed. He said that the *get* represented a "going of our separate ways." It was a real ending—a *psychological divorce*. According to Moshe it was not good if issues within the civil divorce still needed to be worked out. There should be no loose ends. His advice:

> Finish your civil divorce.
> Then do the *get*.

My convictions were affirmed by his words of strength. Even though I sensed what Moshe was going to say, I had to hear the words. I simply needed to know that what I already understood to be right was also in accordance with Jewish law.

A few days later my husband called to tell me he had some new information.

"I spoke to Rabbi Moshe," he said. "He told me that it was okay to do the *get* now."

This did not make sense. I knew what Moshe had said to me. I had asked his advice, and he had suggested that we wait. Did he actually tell my husband something different? We each spoke to him. How could it be that we understood completely divergent responses?

> This was not the first time
> we viewed the world
> with
> a different set of eyes.

It seemed that my husband's only concern was *halakha* (Jewish law), not feelings or closure. I don't think he was interested in what was emotionally best, just what was acceptable according to the ancient rabbis who interpreted the law.

Different views of reality shaped by separate concerns. A steady theme throughout our marriage. Separate experiences on the same physical plane. Always.

We continually battled over right and wrong—his way, my way. When we entertained, I thought the music was too loud. He thought it wasn't loud enough. It seemed as though we were arguing over sound level, but music was not the issue. Our conflict focused on *perceptions of reality.*

His view—my view.

The disagreements were about concerns and interests and the subtle differences we experienced. I was interested in our company being able to *hear each other.* He was interested in our company *hearing the essence of the music.*

Not exactly
a
right/wrong
issue.

The problem was that we never understood the texture of our arguments as we became locked into "I want." As usual my husband and I were standing in the same spot but experiencing different realities. We had been in this place before.

13

Warm Hand
on a Cold Face

Many, many years ago when we were just kids on a beach in San Francisco, I had an experience that became our primal marital metaphor.

It was the sixties
an ethereal
time
with
little to fear
and much to love.

We played on a cold, sunny ocean beach and enjoyed a double hit of window-pane acid that our doctor friends had given us. I had been swimming in the water, which was quite amazing, as the sand was almost too cold to stand on without shoes.

My body was quite cold, and the towel I was wrapped in did not seem to be warming me. The sun was therapeutic and partially warmed the one part of my exposed body: my face. As I stood shivering in the sun, I feared that I would never become warm because, simply, I could not *remember* what warm was.

From a corner of my consciousness I sensed my husband was near. In that moment of comfort and fear, I felt intense, overwhelming love for him. That was when he placed his warm, gentle hand on my cheek. The warmth of his hand on my cold face—well—it was like one giant *ahhhh.* Heat spread through my entire body immediately.

There are no accurate words for that unique instant in time. Anything else I say would degrade the moment. All I know is that I wanted his hand to never move, and the moment to never end.

> We were so young
> and so
> distracted by love.

"What are you feeling?" I asked, as his gentle hand touched my cheek.

"A cold face," was his response with a smile.

I can still feel the sharpness of his concrete words. With disbelief I remember being awed at this synchronistic experience where he and I were in the same moment experiencing the *here and now* from opposite ends of the universe.

> We were standing
> on the same beach
> on the same sand
> in the same sun.
>
> He experienced cold.
> I experienced warmth.

I guess it's a pretty simple concept. Not incredibly profound. An idea that finds expression daily. He wants the covers on. I want the covers off. But for some reason on that beach so long ago, that primal experience struck me in a

profound way. His simple words pushed me away when I
wanted to be close.

He couldn't wait to
pull his hand away.
And I wanted that
moment for eternity.

That one instance on the beach came to represent our
life together and the end of our life together.

He wanted it now.
I wanted it later.

Different desires until the end.

That cold, sunny ocean beach flashed before me as my
husband related his conversation with Reb Moshe.

We must be in San Francisco
I thought to myself.

I will not go into the specifics of the divorce or the settlement process—another story for another time. Let me just say that it was extremely bitter, angry and hurtful. I regularly experienced a stranger. My husband was no longer the one I knew

> in the sun
> on the ocean beach.

I struggled not to think about the past, as my mind raced between tender thoughts and disturbing realities. Over the years we had become quite skilled at hurting each other. We knew exactly where to find the soft spots.

14

Hurtling Toward the End

My husband loved going to movies. So did I. And we were generally in agreement about what to see or what specifically was a great movie. We probably would have both suggested that *Z* was a classic, even though it was difficult to endure. This was another time.

During the last few years as my private practice grew, I was less able to enjoy great movies such as *Kiss of the Spider Woman* or *Fanny and Alexander*. I became drawn to light, entertaining features instead. I worked regularly with trauma, and when it came time to pick a movie, I basically wanted to see Walt Disney.

My husband increasingly lobbied for independent films, art films. Any film was acceptable as long as it was not in English. He came to look down on movies as entertainment.

Once, we had an incredibly angry, hurtful argument that began as a simple discussion about *Indiana Jones and the Last Crusade*. This is the movie in which Indiana Jones attempts to prove himself to his father.

Even though the movie was not a deep intellectual experience, parts could be seen as metaphorical and spiritual. My husband thought the movie was simply a shallow experience.

I felt strongly about a specific scene in the film where Indy, while pursuing the Holy Grail, manages to overcome several death-defying obstacles. He then reaches what seems to be one last insurmountable barrier as he finds himself on the edge of an abyss. Across a chasm, the Grail is in sight, but significantly beyond his reach.

> Indy whispers to himself,
> *"A leap of faith."*

With closed eyes, he jumps into the abyss. Immediately, a light bridge emerges across the chasm, allowing Indy to walk safely to the other side—reaching the Holy Grail.

I was touched emotionally by that unsophisticated scene, as I thought it held a powerful and familiar message about belief and risk. It was a great visual that I brought into the office—showing my patients how one truly must experience an absolute leap of faith before meaningful change can occur. Now this simple scene in a non-subtitled American film became the center of yet another painful disagreement.

We were in therapy again, and for some obscure reason in the midst of one therapy session we began to talk about this movie. During the session, I mentioned that certain scenes had touched me in a profound way. My husband and our therapist then laughed together, as they both agreed that the film was trite and pretty worthless.

The next morning while discussing our therapy session, I told my husband that I had been hurt by what felt like the two of them laughing at me.

Scrunching his face and pursing his lips, he began taunting—in a high, mocking, little-kid voice.

Oh was the iddy biddy little girl hurt?

Instantly, I became flooded with rage as I lost normal consciousness. The pain, anger and humiliation welled up as I ran from the room. I felt violated as I stripped off my clothes, seeking safety and cleansing in the shower.

> Water pounding
> on my fragile body.
> Can it cleanse the wounds
> and heal the
> cavernous hole?

He continued to taunt and mock from an ancient place. I began to howl. A sound came from deep within my soul. A primordial sound from beyond time. Frightening. It was not me who became lost in the cry and so wracked with sobbing.

I sat huddled in the shower, unaware that I had blocked the drain. Water pounded every inch of my body. How long had I been sitting there, shrieking?

Momentarily my consciousness returned as my husband opened the shower door to show me that a great deal of water had flooded out of the shower onto the bathroom carpet. Did I know that was happening? he asked.

I was incapable of response as the water continued to batter my body—unable to relieve the pain.

We learned well over the years. We knew exactly where to poke and prod—so good at bringing the wounds to a place above the skin's surface. It did not take much to create conflict.

Why didn't I know that in my quest for right, we were hurtling toward the end?

He would say something critical. I would withdraw. I would ask for help. He would ignore. I would become angry. He felt justified. I hurt him, too. It built.

> We had such plans
> I could hear our grandchildren call
> *Grandma, Grandpa.*

The gap widened and our lives exhibited a familiar cycle of loving conflict. As the pain subsided and awareness was restored, the feelings of love intensified until the next

conflictual moment and the cycle began again. The intensity
of the pain was balanced by the seductiveness of the love.

I don't know exactly when the obvious became known to
me, but I finally understood. The current struggle, with
memories good and bad, was simply about *continuation* and
the desire to *not end* the marital bond.

> For this man
> I
> fought my father
> hurt a boy
> and
> broke a promise
> to my daughter.

Racing thoughts. Memories. Conflicts. Dishonesty.
Deceit. Broken vows. Angry words. The inventory. How
many more pages of three columns do I write? When will I
be free?

And why was I
now
thinking of
Fairview Road
and listening to
The Who
as the sun rested
on the Flatirons?

He shared love with another today. He wanted me out of
his life. The *get* would serve its purpose.

15

A Date Is Set

I dreaded the arrival of the signed court papers officially signifying the end of our marriage. No one told me that the permanent orders had been sent, and when they arrived in a plain envelope without any message, it was stark.

Alone in my entryway I stared at the unassuming envelope. *Shouldn't there be some fanfare?*

I ripped open the envelope without concern that I might be damaging an original court document. I was anxious to see this official disconnect notice from the city.

> ## DISTRICT COURT,
> ## CITY AND COUNTY OF DENVER
>
> Case No. 99 DR 43, Courtroom 4
> DECREE (DISSOLUTION OF MARRIAGE) . . .
> THIS MATTER was reviewed before the Court. . . .
> the marriage . . . is irretrievably broken. . . . IT IS
> THEREFORE ORDERED, ADJUDGED AND
> DECREED. . . .

I waited for the feelings to surface, but I felt absolutely nothing. I asked myself, "Is this all there is?"

I expected to cry. I expected my heart to pound. I expected to relive our first kiss, our wedding, the birth of our child— but there was nothing. I looked at the final decree from the court and thought

> that's easy
> piece of cake

It was a real surprise.

A few days later my husband called to tell me that the western-sector scribe was going to be in town soon (my first thought was of the Pony Express) and that this was a good time to schedule the *get*. Could we set a date?

The scribe came through Denver several times a year and ran something like a *get* mill. He would schedule as many as possible for one or two days. I had chills at the thought.

Negative emotions dominated and the dark side took over. Weak thoughts permeated the conversation in my head. *This is not my ritual. It has no significance. Let them do it without me. That's what they want. My husband would be pleased. He only wants a piece of paper.*

I have to admit there was a big part of me that just wanted to walk—take the easy way out. Call up the west-side rabbi, give him the information he asked for, the okay, and then it would be done. No humiliation, no fear and no men who did not see me as existing in the scheme of life. No severing. No cutting. No pain. Wouldn't that really be simpler?

Words of Stephen Covey resonated. "Our most difficult experiences become the crucibles that forge our character and develop . . . freedom." Easy for him to say—I fought back in a defensive, reactive moment. The internal battle raged, as the temptation to *not do* the right thing became evident.

I had to remain focused and cognizant of what Reb Kalman had said about a "powerful experience." And mindful of Reb Moshe and his encouraging words: "A real ending and closure." The ritual was necessary. I really did not want to be eighty years old and still emotionally connected to my husband.

We agreed on a date. It was done.

I called Reb Moshe and told him that we had set a date. I asked him if the time was a good time for him. Could he be at the west-side *shul* on that date? Was that going to work out for him?

My mind raced—fueled by fear.

I told him that I needed to know because my husband was making arrangements with the scribe right now and if he couldn't be there on that date I wanted to call my husband back and tell him we were going to have to find another time, and I thought that would be okay because I remember my husband saying that the scribe was going to be in town for a few days and I was sure that we could come up with another date that worked for everybody—if this time wasn't good.

"The date works for me," he said without hesitation.

When I heard his response, anxiety surfaced immediately as I became drenched in fearful thoughts and images. How do I handle the noise in my head and the sound of my racing heart? The computerized Times Square moving message flashed above my head. *No more stalling. . . . This is it. . . . No way out.*

Reb Moshe again suggested a joint meeting prior to the *get*. He wanted the two of us together when we heard his vital last-minute instructions. "It's part of the process," he said.

Coming together
before

ripping apart

is

necessary.

The beginning of the experience was facing the end together, but my husband chose another way—never meeting with Reb Moshe in preparation for the end.

The date was set. The path toward the inevitable had been readied. I had felt nothing when the court papers arrived, but at this moment my heart beat loudly outside my chest.

Until now, I had little awareness that my defenses were so strong or that my fear was so great.

Reb Moshe was expecting me, maybe even looking forward to our meeting. I was not. What an irreverent thought, as meeting with Moshe had always been special— his time so precious.

During this meeting at his *shul* he was very gentle and thorough. He understood the ritual all too well and he wanted it to be good for me, as did Reb Kalman. I was very lucky.

Moshe knew how difficult it was for me to listen to the description of the process that would end my marriage. It was like listening to a skilled surgeon describe operating procedures prior to surgery. Only this surgeon was planning to kill the patient.

Moshe spent several hours with me. Going over every conceivable detail of writing, giving and receiving the *get*. He was meticulous in his descriptions and explanations.

> I did not know at the time
> what a gift he was offering.

Moshe repeated the information over and over again. Slowly. Gently. Patiently.

"Do you have any questions? Are you sure? Do you understand? Do you know why they will ask you that? Do you want to know why it is called a *get*? Would you like to see a completed *get*? Do you have any more questions?"

> This was remote
> foreign
> and
> I could feel the fear
> in my throat
> on my skin
> in my belly.

Incredible heaviness in the Rabbi's study
as I began to deal with my dishonest self.

Toward the end of our time together, Rabbi Moshe suggested that I consider bringing someone else along for the
meeting with the rabbinic panel. Even though Moshe was
going to be present, he thought that it might be good to
have a friend take me. He was concerned about me driving.

Several friends actually offered, but I was reluctant to
have them join me. I sensed the intensity of the experience
more and more, and I couldn't imagine asking a friend to go
through that.

Why don't you come with me tomorrow
while I have my guts ripped out?

It felt harsh at the time, but I decided not to have anyone
join me. Instead, I asked Reb Moshe if he would drive me
to the Orthodox *shul* on the west side of town. He said
he would. So ironic. Back to the neighborhood where it

all began. Stark contrast, then and now. But this is today's west side

> where the scribe will do the writing
> on the parchment.

We arranged to meet at his *shul* at about noon and then drive from there to the west side. It was all set. Simple. Nothing to prepare. Just be there.

16

Crossing the Threshold

I believe the plan was to meet Reb Moshe at noon. I cannot tell you for sure, as many of the day's experiences are less than sharp. Sadly, some are vivid, solid, gelled-forever memories.

I don't remember driving to Reb Moshe's *shul* or meeting him or getting into his huge old car. I remember joking about the size of the front seat. He has a big family.

I don't remember the ride or what we talked about. I

don't remember the neighborhoods we drove through or the businesses we passed. I do recall thinking to myself that I never could have made this drive alone.

When we arrived at the old west-side *shul,* Moshe was greeted by a rabbi he knew. They seemed happy to see each other as they hugged and laughed. I expected to meet no one familiar in this part of town, and for a moment I resented their pleasure in being together. I walked ahead down the sidewalk—alone.

As I approached the door of the *shul,* I was stunned by graffiti on the walls and doors. Skinheads had spray painted the *shul* the night before.

In order to enter the building, I had to place my hand on a door defiled by a large swastika. The words above read

DIE JEWS

I did not think about the enormity of those words scrawled in scarlet red paint. I had only self-centered thoughts. *Great. This could not be happening. I am going to my get. What is graffiti doing here?*

I had never before experienced anti-Semitic graffiti. In fact, the angry little girl who yelled at me when I was in first grade was pretty much the extent of my contact with Jewish hate. Was this an omen not to enter? The symbolism was almost sophomoric. It jolted my consciousness as I began a rapid internal dialogue. *Apparently, we need to reschedule. This clearly is not the right day. I have to tell Moshe that we will return some other time.*

As I crossed the threshold to enter the *shul,* I wondered what the angry scribbling meant. Did I truly not belong here? Did it have to be so hard until the end?

Obviously
nothing easy here.

At this moment I would not have felt the pain of a knife plunging through my chest. Numb and detached I have no memory of walking through the door. I do recall suddenly seeing my husband and being shocked by his presence. I had forgotten my mission for that day. "Why is he here?" I thought to myself, and then I remembered.

Slugged by a tidal wave of grief, my memory jolted me. You know, like after someone special has died. The feeling you have when you suddenly think about that person. It's as though, for a moment, you actually forgot the person has died. Then—*wham*—the memory returns, shakes your consciousness and the sadness resurfaces. He's gone.

I didn't cry at first when I was told that my father had died suddenly. I received the information about his death over the telephone and immediately began preparations for the trip back to Chicago.

> I did the laundry.
> I cleaned the house.
> I watered the plants.

I arranged for child care.
But I didn't cry.

I remember lying in bed that first night in Chicago, at my sister's, when a realization hit me.

My father will never see my daughter swim.

Such a silly thought
at
such a significant time.

She was two and a half and swimming the width of the pool. I was so proud. It seemed so natural. Her grandfather Augie loved the water. He would go off by himself and swim for hours, disappearing into the seemingly infinite water of Lake Michigan. My mother always worried, but Augie said he could think better after a good swim—that the water soothed him. Swimming was his passion.

When the thought hit me that my father would never see his grandchild swim that width, just once—it stung. In my throat and eyes and head. I was pounded and flooded with emotion.

My husband was in the back of the sanctuary reading or praying. I could not tell which. He glanced up at me with a familiar look, an uncomfortable half smile. He did not look good. Has he been taking care of himself? I wondered.

It was dark in the sanctuary, but some light filtered through a small high window. The light caught the dust and debris that occupied this old building. The feeling was one of unreality. Let's call it an out-of-body experience.

> I was watching
>
> me
>
> observe my husband.

I protested. This is not happening. I am not here. I am not ending my marriage. We signed an agreement—*until death do us part.* This is not right. We can't be here to fulfill a commandment of the Torah.

> *And he shall write her*
>
> *a*
>
> *bill of divorcement.*

With the first glimpse of my husband sitting in that far corner of the sanctuary, the emotion surfaced. It surrounded my skin. For a moment my body moved involuntarily.

> I knew we were approaching
> the end.
> I could
> feel it now.
> He looked so sad.

My mind raced. Why was this happening? Could we somehow begin again? It was not too late. We could learn from our mistakes.

> I shouted *stop*
> but
> no one heard.

I didn't decide to get divorced. We never talked about it. It just happened. We separated. He met someone. We got attorneys. It was done. How did I wind up alone in a dark old *shul* covered with graffiti, about to participate in an archaic ritual that ignores women and ends marriage? I didn't write this script. I didn't want this ending. I wasn't ready. I wanted to run or scream, or both.

The scribe was not ready to begin because not everyone had arrived. I experienced relief as I walked outside and felt the crisp air. Sharp was the contrast between the dark interior and the bright light outside.

I flashed on being a little kid leaving the Saturday afternoon movie matinee at the Granada Theater. Walking from the black theater into the harsh white light. You know where you just push open the theater door and walk outside. The light stings your eyes.

My eyes remained filled with tears as I walked outside to the back of the building. A Channel 9 TV news reporter stood with a film crew getting shots of the angry messages on the brick walls.

I could see it now—"Film at ten." Was this really happening? Or was I tragically caught in the twilight zone with a Rod Serling look-alike about to greet me?

The TV reporter and I spoke briefly. We talked of the graffiti and its significance. The reporter shared with me that he was Jewish and concerned.

"Why are you here?" he asked.

My voice cracked.

I'm here to end my marriage.

I'm ending my marriage and you're filming a news shoot. We both might end up on the cutting-room floor tonight, as Paddy Chayefsky pens this scene.

I walked back into the building and glanced at my husband. He showed that all-too-familiar half-strained smile again. He too looked as though he had been crying. His eyes were red and glassy.

I wanted him to hold me and tell me that this was not happening. That we could go back to the beach when we were kids and the sun was warm and his hand felt good on my face. I wanted him to tell me that everything would be okay and we could start again.

No words passed between us.

I walked into the rabbi's study, where I was introduced to the scribe and told to be seated. Books dominated this small room, as did a huge oversized desk, spanning almost wall to wall.

The scribe did not fit in this room. The other men were black hats, all speaking Yiddish. Long dark beards, black hats and fringes—not my world. I loved Reb Moshe. I never felt like an outsider with him. But this was not my place. I was not even visible to the eye.

The scribe was wearing a handsome, costly suit. I wanted to tell him that I liked his tie. He had magnificent white hair, immaculately coifed. His skin was tanned. His hands were smooth and unblemished. No wrinkles. Physically he was trim and good looking. If I passed him on the street I would have thought, "Sharp . . . worldly. He knows how to pick a good wine." He didn't fit in this ancient room.

Books everywhere, piled to the ceiling and in all directions, vertically, horizontally, diagonally. Papers were shoved in corners. There was almost no empty space in this room. Ancient clutter. You could see the dust floating in the air as the light caught specks of history.

The black hats were ultra-Orthodox rabbis. But not like

Reb Moshe. You felt good about yourself when you were with him. With these other men I felt insignificant. It was a struggle to maintain my presence. My existence.

The scribe was from another place. He traveled the circuit, and this was his time to come through my town. He was here to write our final chapter.

17

The Rabbi's Study

I don't think I was introduced to the other learned men in the room. I know my husband was. There was a camaraderie among them immediately, as they joked with each other on the far side of the room. I distinctly felt like the *other*. After all, I was the only one in this room who preferred the toilet seat down.

> My heart pounded
> and
> I began to sweat.
> *I never sweat,* I thought.

What was it Kalman had said to me?
Why didn't I ask more questions?

I am used to public speaking. I am comfortable asserting myself in the midst of strangers. I do not intimidate. I am solid and self-assured. A bit on the cocky side at times. I don't become frightened in front of people. But I was scared when I sensed my powerless stature.

> *Like clay in the hands*
> *of the potter.*

The only way I can explain it is that I suddenly felt as though I were an American citizen alone in Iraq and government officials were walking me down to a dark basement room where they began questioning me about why I didn't have a passport or any other identification—and what was this white powdery substance they had found in my backpack?

> It was scary.
> This was not my country.

I recall feeling frozen, afraid to move or talk. I felt like I couldn't ask questions or get out of my seat until given permission. I didn't understand the language and it was obvious that it mattered to no one, except Reb Moshe, that I was there. Most in the room seemed annoyed by my presence.

> I am ten years old at a new school
> on the first day and
> I'm wearing the wrong clothes.
> The boys on the other side of the room
> are pointing and laughing.

The black hats are in a corner to the left of me, laughing. I imagine them saying, "What is she doing here? She's just in the way. Why would she want to be here? Tell her she can leave."

I sat down in a chair directly in front of the scribe and his huge empty desk. My husband sat down in a chair next to me, to the left. We were side by side in front of the scribe. To the left of us at the far edge of the desk were the two rabbis (the black hats) who would gather the information and do the checking for accuracy.

A few specific items were on the desk. A telephone, a piece of white parchment and two small glasses.

Plain, clear, water glasses, like the ones from old 1950s restaurants with Formica tables. I-must-be-in-Woolworth's glasses. One glass had some black ink at the bottom. The other held just a bit of water and four or five turkey quills. *These glasses were not grand enough to hold those special quills and ink.*

The telephone was to the left of the scribe, and the ink, quills and parchment were directly in front of him. He was ready to write. An artist with his tools.

> But this was a
> Rembrandt,
> not a
> Renoir.

The black hats were still laughing and speaking Yiddish. A scream bloated my head. *Why are they laughing at my funeral? Where was their sensitivity to an experience that defied explanation?* This moment that transcended time—sitting really still and listening to the grass as it grows. *The Golden Apple,* a vivid childhood memory. Those wonderful, magical summer nights under the theater tent. Time was slower then. Not like now. Today I wasn't able to stop the rapid intrusion and flooding of thoughts.

The black hats huddled next to each other like school-boys telling dirty jokes. They spoke some Yiddish to my husband, but soon it became apparent to them that he did not understand. It was then that they decided to speak in English.

> The questions began
> slowly
> over and over
> again and again
> the same questions
> as before.

First to my husband. Always first to him.

"Are you giving the *get* freely? What is your name? What did your parents call you? What else did they call you? What other names were you called? Are there any other names that you have been called? What is your father's name? What other names was he called? Are there any other names that your father was called?"

I sat motionless and silent.

Again and again. They asked the same exact questions.

They must have spent twenty minutes or so with my husband. Then it was my turn to respond.

"Are you accepting the *get* of your own free will? What is your name? What did your parents call you? What other names were you called?"

In the midst of this questioning, to add a bizarre twist, the scribe had to answer the telephone. He accomplished this by writing with his right hand and holding the telephone with his left hand.

It is the press. TV news and print media. They want to know about the graffiti. The scribe knows nothing. He is not even sure of the name of the *shul*. He has just been transported from another time and place. But he is very courteous and jovial on the telephone. He is comfortable with life.

> As he laughs and jokes
> my insides break apart.

The tension is thick as the questions continue. "What is your father's name?" I was asked again. "Alan," I answered. The tears struck again. I was not prepared to be sad thinking about my father. Tears at the thought of my father? The one who never wanted this marriage.

He never wanted me to marry this person sitting next to

me, and he was probably at this moment shaking his finger from afar. He wanted me to marry the other boy, the one he had grown so fond of.

There was something almost laughable about the interruption by the press and the questioning about my father. Yes, Augie would have liked this. And my husband knew that too.

"What other names was he called?"

"Augie," responded my husband.

No one seemed to notice that my husband had answered for me. "Augie?" asked the scribe with a look of disbelief. As though he had never heard the name before. Or maybe he thought it was an odd name for a Jewish male.

"He was probably called Augie more often than anything else," explained my husband.

Only *he* would know this.

The strangers in this room knew nothing of my father. And why didn't they want to know about the little blonde lady? No questions were asked about this special woman who gave me life. The one who loved the sun.

My husband understood this woman. He once said to

me, early in our marriage, "You know, getting along with
your mom is pretty simple. All you have to do is be nice to
her."

> The magic key to
> acceptability.
> Betty's litmus test.

More tears. I did not want to cry. I had not planned for
this. The sadness was gripping.

> This one
> who remembered Augie and Betty
> was being cut from me.

We were the ones in the room with the history. We
shared the common memories. My husband was the one
who would remember the awful letter about the "no talk
suit."

My father was angry at our plans to marry. Too young
and marrying the wrong boy were high on his list of com-
plaints. We didn't have jobs. Law school was still a question
mark. I had to be the breadwinner. Support my husband?

The concept was very foreign and upsetting to my father as well as my mother.

> *I raised you*
> *to be taken care of*
> *in grand style,*
> my mother would say.

Discussions about a wedding were not going very well. This was not what my parents had planned or hoped for. I had chosen someone to marry, and my father basically said, "No."

That had never happened before. I had never gone against anything my father suggested. I idolized him. He could do no wrong in my eyes. I had the perfect father. Now I was challenging him for the first time. He was making me choose.

My father just decided that if communication stopped, so would the marriage. With no talking, there would be no plans and of course there could be no wedding. My father basically became silent. Except for comments like "Please pass the butter."

Before my college graduation, my father wished to set the tone of our celebration weekend. He told me that his communication ground rules were not going to change just because this was a happy get-together.

He wrote a lengthy, sardonic letter—the "no talk suit" letter—explaining that at graduation he would be wearing a suit specially made for the occasion. He wanted me to know that if I attempted to talk to him about anything besides the weather, his suit would automatically disintegrate. The scribe didn't know that.

> So incredibly alone
> at this moment of memory.
> Until I reasoned a friend is here.
> He knows of my life.

There was something so tender and connected yet painfully tragic as the two of us ended our life together speaking of my father.

> The one who caused us
> both
> so much pain.

My husband, who as the years passed had grown close to my father, explained to this stranger with the pen that Augie was a more comfortable name than Alan or Abe or Abraham.

> Was anybody listening . . .
> did anybody care?
> Memories compounded
> along with the tears.

My parents, my husband, me, our young child. Good times. Special times. How sad he was when Augie died, the only father he had really known. More tears and shared memories. Nixon and a holiday card. An incredible bottle of Mouton-Rothschild. Walking through deep mountain snow. Images flashing.

Calm, motionless exterior, with shrieking insides. *You are not writing a traffic ticket,* I wanted to shout. *This is my life you are dissecting. Where is the compassion—the morality, the sanctity?*

Something was terribly wrong with this moment. These intimate, painful memories in the midst of men who didn't care. Just another day's work in this cold, dark, cluttered room, as a paper document holds more importance than human flesh.

Form over substance.

The phone rang again and again. More press. More
inquiries. A steady stream of people walking in and out of
this small room, asking questions. The sprinkler repairman
wanted to know where the turn-on valve was. He asked the
scribe for its location.

I wanted to get everyone's attention in order to scream....

> *Wait.*
> *This ... is ... a*
> *private ... moment.*
> I shouted silently
> inside.
> *We are ending*
> *our life together.*

A woman, unknown to me, peeks in from the other
room. She is the next in line. She has come from forty miles
away—and eleven years. It has taken her that long to obtain
consent from her husband so she can have the *get* written.

She tells me her story with pride. He lives far away and
has no interest in the process. It means a great deal to her.

She is relieved that he has finally consented.

I glance at her and think for a moment that she is yet another stranger violating the intimacy of a life together. It doesn't concern me that her eyes focus on our ending. She is just one more to invade this sanctuary.

My breathing is shallow. I'm not sure I have to breathe. I am cemented to the process in this room. I cannot take my eyes from the scribe. I am simply transfixed as he cautiously draws each letter. I cannot get enough of this moment.

> Slowly
> every word
> must be correct
> every letter
> must be precise
> exact.

The black hats each handwrite in Hebrew our responses to the questions, and the scribe then uses these exact words to write on his parchment. Did Lanzmann script this? The black hats . . .

        they do not look at me

        as

        I am not counted in their

        scheme of life.

Emotional flooding at this moment explains why I am not bothered by their insensitivity. Something that would normally cause me to kick and scream creates a non-response in me.

There is such intensity in this small space, it simply doesn't matter at this point in time. Their eyes are of no concern to me. These learned men are mere puppets in this powerful play. I know that now.

The questions are asked again and again. They become a mantra in my meditation.

Reminiscent of the Sufi dancers I observed many years ago in Boulder. Twirling endlessly again and again. *No. They are not all going to twirl that way. Not each of them. Again?*

        Long ago

        the monotony of it all.

Only *I*
was bored by this unique experience.
Only *I*
could not see the spirituality
in their profound
repetitive
movement.

Such a heaviness in the room. Was it the grief? You could feel the walls. And the stories they had to tell. How many fathers' names had been repeated in this room before?

It was as though the room were underwater and we were experiencing this process—beneath the sea. Only the seawater was more like oil. The weight in this room created thick air and a musty smell.

When had they opened a window last?

The questioning continued for about an hour. "What city do you live in? What river runs through it? Is there other water close by? What are some other cities nearby?" The location needs to be exact. There can be no confusing my *get* with someone else's *get*.

The questions are tedious. But I don't mind. I don't want them to ever end. I don't want these men to ever stop asking questions. I don't want the woman outside to be sitting where I am sitting. This is my turn now.

It doesn't matter that for every ten questions they ask my husband, they ask me two. Or that they look at my husband when they speak and do not look at me. The power of the moment compensates.

In this room we experience abnormal time and space. Words are fluid—thick. Movements are like pieces of apple falling through a honey jar. Slow. Slower than slow. It is like I am watching someone paint us.

The scribe is not from this place—he is clearly a visitor. He does glance up every once in a while as he makes notes. He says a few words to me. For example, he explains why the heavy black lines will be drawn on the blank parchment.

His rules are different.

Finally the questions are done. The black hats have the required information on their papers. They must be satisfied. Every word must be correct. They compare their notes, carefully.

Each word has to be the same. Each response has to be exact. No mistakes are allowed. One mistake would require the entire document to be rewritten. It has to be perfect.

The document is correct, they say. It is time for the scribe to *really* begin his work.

18

Writing the *Get*

Light passed through the high window again, catching everything in the air. Do we really breathe that? Pieces of life floated upward toward the ceiling. How could there be so much stuff in the air?

The black hats departed for now, along with Reb Moshe. Strange when I think about it: I had no awareness of Moshe's presence. I did not see him. I can't even tell you where he was sitting. He did not participate in the questioning, yet I know he was in the room. I simply felt his presence—his warmth and protection. That was all that was necessary.

The scribe explained quietly that he was ready. He could begin to write the document, and—if we wanted—we could leave. It was going to take him about forty-five minutes to complete the writing.

My husband stood up and asked where he could find a telephone. He said he needed to call his office. It was clear that he was in another place. He appeared distracted.

> *Leave?* I thought.
> *This is my last connection.*

> I sit glued to my chair
> in the midst of a
> meditation on my life.

I watch the scribe fold his blank parchment several times and then slowly and methodically draw perfect black lines on the paper. The heavy black lines on the white parchment are necessary to ensure that the document can never be changed or altered.

Every letter has to be bisected by a heavy black line. This

protects against forgery or adulteration. There can be no modification of letters or words.

> This document is forever
> and ever.

A long time ago, I read one of the Adam Smith books, *Powers of Mind.* One chapter I have never forgotten deals with the belief that there are things that can't be photographed. I loved that thought. It so perfectly described the concept that some experiences just don't lend themselves to verbal descriptions. This was one of those experiences.

I liked the way the scribe looked at me and talked to me, acknowledging my existence. His eyes had that look. "High eyes" we called it in the sixties. I liked him. He took time to talk to me and explain what he was doing. It intensified the experience for me and it brought me comfort.

Outside this space a rushed and frantic world waited its turn. Somehow this writer of endings carved out a temple of calm. He did not rush, he worked in his own sphere of time—one not regulated by a clock. He seemed not to care that he had many more documents to pen that day.

On this day
he is honoring
my special parchment.

Again he said, "You can leave if you want. It will be a while before I finish."

I was transfixed. The writing was something from long ago. An ancient ritual—in the here and now. And I was the only one left to watch.

The scribe first chose a quill that he dipped in the ink glass, deliberately and cautiously. He tapped the quill a few times against the inside edge of the small glass, until he had just the right amount of ink. I watched the excess ink slowly drip down the inside of the glass where it joined the black pool at the bottom. He knew exactly how much ink he needed.

He used one quill for a moment, then returned it to the glass. One of his fingers jostled the quills from side to side as they rested in the glass. He paused for an instant as he decided which quill to pick up. I wish I would have asked him how he knew which quill to use.

He formed each letter slowly. Each letter carefully. Exactly. With precision. Writing from right to left. Hebrew letters. The letters of the Bible. God's letters on my document. *Black fire on white fire.*

I became lost in his precision and do not know how long I focused on the parchment and those sharp letters. But I knew soon the writing would be complete. The group would reconvene.

Too fast. This is going too quickly. It can't end. Not yet. I'm not ready. We were happy long ago.

> *Valorous wife*
> *far greater*
> *than pearls.*

I was forgetting the hurt and the pain and the anger. Our life together was precious. I remembered no black spots at this moment.

We sure were cocky, believing that it could never end. So much taken for granted. Why didn't I treasure what we had? The perfect life, some thought. I had regrets. I should have been more careful. It seems so obvious now. When did we stop paying attention? How could we have let the love slip away?

We walked in the wind with passion—not touching—just experiencing the intensity and power of the moment, which lasted a lifetime.

It was magic.
Couldn't he remember?

My husband returned. He peeked into the room, checking on the progress of the scribe. He appeared impatient and anxious. His body was positioned in the doorway, but his thoughts were definitely somewhere else.

The author at the desk presented a distinct contrast, as he methodically penned our life script. After all, he was the one writing and directing this final scene. No distractions here.

"How are we doing?" my husband asked.

"Just a few more minutes," answered the scribe.

I smelled the leaves from that crisp October day near Varsity Lake in Boulder. Glistening reds and yellows sticking to our feet. This special ground cover, crunching and dancing in the wind. We made a promise with our eyes.

> Was I the only one . . .
> who had the memories
> and felt the pain
> at this moment?
> Silently I broke in two.

My guts hung out as this stranger in the elegant suit wrote the end. What did he know about painful nights of terror and calming moments in bed? What did he know about the rock or a river of water under the concrete slab? Or Mr. Dickery—who made the mistake of running his car off the road in front of our Cherryvale Road house. All this lost soul wanted was the use of a telephone.

Intrusive memories resonated in my head. King Vidor films, *Help, I'm a Rock,* the smell of marijuana mixed with tear gas and Jimi Hendrix on a hot summer night. Majestic Prince Arn lying on a table in the vet's office, driving to Ram Dass in the snow. And remember when Osa ate the couch? Did my life partner recall these things, or was I truly alone in this dark, musty room?

The wait was similar to waiting in the family room at St. Luke's. Waiting for the surgeon to tell us the news we already knew. It was malignant, had spread throughout her body, and the surgeons could do nothing. The wait was endless. Each time the phone rang we jumped. Augie was there then. His precious lover was being taken away.

This wait was endless too, reminiscent of a distinctly separate reality. An altered kind of time. Not necessarily timeless but something immeasurable, and beyond ordinary counting. Longer. Like waiting until Monday for the results of a biopsy, only it was now Friday. The weekend became eternal.

At this infinite moment of illusive time, things were happening too quickly. That was my complaint. Soon it would be done. He would say the ink had dried and it was time to end.

My life as wife and partner would be finished. No more socks on the floor. Why did I complain? No more drawers left half open? Was it really so awful? No more craziness in the middle of the night. No more soft touches. No more poems. No more love notes left on the dresser drawer. And was I never to hear that I was long, lean and lanky again?

> What was I doing?
> This just did not make any sense.
> It was bad.
> There—
> I said it.

We needed to end it. Why was I being so morbid? Why so maudlin? The tension had been unbearable. The chasm had grown. We used to know what the other was thinking. Suddenly we weren't so sure we cared. Why was I being so sentimental now that it was finally over?

> Why couldn't I just let go?

The civil divorce decree had been signed weeks earlier. No sentimental thoughts then. Legally we were not married now. But I felt no different. If he were sick, I would still worry.

> I remained definitely attached
> and

> unwilling to disengage
> emotionally.

The sadness kept me tied. It felt good. Like scratching an itch until it bleeds. It stings but feels sort of good at the same time.

> Of course
> I was enjoying
> the sadness,
> my last connection
> to
> him.

19

Again the Questions

Soon everyone had returned. We settled in our assigned seats. There was something comfortable in this room now. My husband joked with the rabbis. I cannot remember about what.

The document was written. The twelve lines completed. Now for the examination. Each word checked and rechecked by the men in black. They had to make sure that the scribe had written exactly what we had said.

> Word for word
> no mistakes
> no errors
> no inaccuracies.

Got to get it right. Or . . . it . . . all . . . has . . . to . . . be . . . done . . . over.

I want to grab the parchment and rip it into a thousand pieces. *Too bad. You have to begin again. We will return another day.* I will do anything to prolong the inevitable—but I do nothing. The document is correct. The scribe and the rabbis are satisfied.

Overwhelming dread blocks out my consciousness. I remember only the folding and the cutting as I sit in front of the desk.

The scribe meticulously folds the written document. He carefully creases it in half. Then again and again and again, until there remains one folded piece, about one inch by twelve inches.

He grasps one end of the folded parchment in each hand and carefully fits one end into the other—in such a way as to connect the two ends.

Then there is one last fold.

Now the document looks like a little square. Something that a third grade boy would create and then throw at the girl across the room. This is not something that represents the ending of a life together. It is too simple and just too small.

The folding is done.

The scribe then asks us both to stand. It is an awkward moment as we both fumble while getting out of our chairs. Seemed simple enough. But we had been sitting so close to the desk and to each other that when it was time to get up we almost fell over our chairs. There wasn't enough room for us to stand between the chair and the desk. So we had to stand and then push back our chairs and walk behind them. It should have been a simple movement, but it was not.

The three of us stood very close together. Like a football huddle, only smaller. The scribe in front of me, slightly off to my right. My husband, directly to my left.

> My only awareness
> was of the
> scribe
> and his words.

He asked us each again. First was my husband giving the *get* freely, and then was I accepting the *get* of my own free will? He had to make sure, one last time. He then told me to cup my hands, and to hold my hands out in front of me. I imagined I was using my hands to catch precious water for a parched throat.

I cupped my hands and became vigilant, watchful for a delicate object about to be dropped into them.

> *Can't let it*
> *fall through*
> I thought to myself.

I stood there mesmerized and motionless. I could not move or hear or think or breathe. Consuming awareness. Heart pulsing in my head—like the piercing drill in the movie *The Big Carnival.* My eyes rigidly glaring only at my fixed hands as the questions to my husband began again.

> The questions,
> the same questions.
> Are the Sufis twirling?

How silly I must have appeared. Why didn't I just look up? I could have turned slightly to glance at my husband. Who told me to stare at my hands?

I wish I would have seen his face. What did his eyes say? Why didn't I look to see? Was there pain or relief? Were his eyes filled with tears as mine were?

> I will never know.
> The opportunity to know
> was lost—forever.

The questions again to my husband, not to me. The scribe asks the questions over and over. The same questions. *Not again!* I scream a silent scream. *Don't you know the answers?*

He must have heard my noisy head because the scribe paused, turned to me and said, "I want you to listen carefully. When I am through with the questions, I will hand you the document. I want you to then give it to your husband. He is going to drop it into ... your ... hands as he speaks the words that will cut you from him. At the exact moment that it touches your hands, you are to close your cupped hands together tightly. When your hands are closed together ...

> *you ... will ... not ... be ...*
> *married ... anymore."*

I can still feel those
words

throughout my body
in every pore
penetrating
and
overwhelming emotion
immediately.

At that exact moment I felt the end.

the ripping
the loss
the emptiness
the isolation
the finality

The scribe turned to my husband and began the questions, only to him. Again. The same questions repeated over and over, one by one. Slowly. Only now they do not bother me.

The three of us stood extremely close. Almost touching. Well, maybe touching. I couldn't be sure. The boundaries were blurred. The questions again: "What is your name? What is your father's name? What else was your father called?"

The experience is disassociative, as I observe myself positioned in some other reality. This is not happening to me. I am not here. This is not me in this room. I am merely an observer of strange events. Looking down from somewhere else. Looking down at someone else.

> Time did stop
> as the air is sucked out
> of the room.
> But that is okay.
> I do not have to breathe.

I am alone in the room, experiencing an altered consciousness. In the distance are the faint, piercing questions of the scribe. But I cannot hear them. My eyes remain fixed on my hands. My thoughts race in unkind directions. There is no escaping the inevitable. I must close my hands the moment my husband drops the *get* into them.

> Vigilant I am.
> I must be
> ready
> to bring my hands
> together
> immediately.

No options here. This is not a time for choices. The choices were made a long time ago. We had our chance.

The questions continue, while I have this odd conversation with myself. *How will I know to be ready?*

> I'm not looking and
> I can't hear the questions
> with all the noise in my head.

Not once did I look up, poised like a racer, anxious for the gun. I had one singular thought.

> I had to
> close my hands
> the instant the document
> touched them.

I don't remember signing the document. I don't remember my husband's words to me or him dropping the folded piece of parchment into my palms. I don't remember the document touching my skin. I didn't see it fall, or feel it.

All I know is that *I closed my hands.*

I was the executioner.
I had thrown the switch.
It was over in an
instant
and an
eternity.
Simultaneously.

And it was my doing.

Psychic surgery. He was cut from me. Torn from my flesh. I was not a wife. I did not have a husband partner. No longer connected—no longer married. I check different boxes on the forms now.

No *Woman of Valor* prayer for me.

The pain becomes overwhelming—feelings defy imagination. The breath is taken from me, as grief invades my body. Animated tears have their own life.

The sensations are
beyond words and ordinary time.

From being a child
to being an adult.
From that first night
and
I want to hold your hand.
From the Beach Boys
to the Beatles
to Beethoven.
I was no longer married.
In one eternal moment
it was done.
Profound Closure.

20

Dirt on the Coffin

I attempt to listen to the scribe's final instructions, a difficult task as I struggle to remain conscious. I am asked to walk across the room and back. My legs have no strength, but they do what they are told.

The document is then taken from me.

> I did not want
> to let it go,
> transitional object
> that it was.

Of course he would take from me
this last connection.
Additional procedures
to get the point across.
As if to say,
If you missed the last part—well—
we want to make sure that you understand.
You are no longer husband and wife.

I listen to the bizarre announcement in my head as I
notice the scribe, from a corner of my eye, reach for the
scissors.

A slice is made
into the
document
he so carefully
penned.
I can still feel
the cut.

I am informed that I cannot marry for ninety days. Only
I am told this. Then the scribe hands us each a ritual offer-
ing. I am given a piece of paper verifying that the *get* has
been written. He is given the scribe's writing instruments.

I do not remember what happened next. The memory truly is lost. It probably never solidified. There is that theory of trauma, you know.

I do believe that I came to know in that instant when it was done why I had not brought a friend. It seemed so clear, as hard as it was. I needed to be alone with the pain and the gripping sadness. I needed to stay present, in the here and now. It was important that nothing should draw me back into feeling connected. I had to remain with the hurtful emotions until their work was done.

> No making this process
> easier.
> Not this time.

This was dirt on the coffin as I reached down to pick up the shovel. I listened to hear the dirt hit the pine box. I had buried my marriage.

I did not have the energy or the steadiness to walk. I never could have driven a car. I could barely find the doorway. I do not remember walking out, saying good-bye or talking to anyone. I vaguely recall passing the woman who was sitting in the hall. She had been waiting a long time to enter this room.

No words passed between me and the man with whom I had shared a life. We walked from the still darkness into the jolting light. We walked through the door, past the graffiti, down the sidewalk toward the huge old car. No words were exchanged as we turned our separate ways. The man I was no longer connected to,

> he walked to the right
> and I walked to the left.

Part II

After the *Get*

21

The Ride Home

I wish I knew what happened after the walk to the car. I don't remember much except being struck by the obvious metaphor. Again that quality of "me watching me" as I observed us move toward separate cars. *This was day surgery*, I thought. Walking continued to be difficult.

No memory exists of getting into the car with Reb Moshe. *Did I open the door or did he?* The feeling was similar to other post-burial rides, like when my parents died. Physical and emotional exhaustion laced with separation from the world. I felt beat up. Like going ten rounds with Sonny Liston. My only desire was for sleep.

We continued to move through *"get* time" in this altered state, as I felt the air pressing against the windows of the car. Few words passed between us during this very quiet, intense ride. Conversation would have been an intrusion. Moshe understood. This was not his first *get*.

It is difficult to imagine an experience that sucks the emotional energy so completely. *How could they be so wrong?* I screamed silently as obsolete dialogs resounded in my head.

> *Piece of cake.*
> *It just takes*
> *a few minutes.*
> *Simple.*

And what could explain the man just cut from me driving back to his office?

> Ignition key,
> a slight turn,
> could not imagine
> unless
> *his* experience
> was
> very different.

✺ ✺ ✺

I don't remember leaving Moshe's car and entering
mine. No awareness of movement in this trancelike state.
Just a short distance separates Moshe's *shul* and my new
home. It was good that my car knew the way. One imprint
of my drive remains. It was slow.

> Something-must-be-
> wrong-
> with-the-car slow
> a stoned slow
> will-the-brownies-
> ever-get-done
> slow.

I could have been ticketed for driving too far below the
thirty-miles-per-hour limit. I don't know what I would
have explained to the officer. The experience was like crawl-
ing over Loveland Pass in a blinding snowstorm. My fingers squeezed the steering wheel as I pointed the vehicle,
hopefully, in the right direction. Only I saw the swirling
wind and snow outside my car.

I do not remember going through stoplights, stop signs or
turning corners. I have no memory of parking or exiting the
car. There remains simply one sustained feeling of disconnection from the world as I walked toward the front door alone.

I thought about going through the turquoise-blue door from my past life as this new life door closed behind me. What a sound. Not the door, the inside. The quiet, sound-less interior.

I don't think I have ever felt so incredibly alone—and frightened. *I am an astronaut securely tethered to a space capsule orbiting beyond the earth's atmosphere. Suddenly there is no connection and I float away into endless light-absent space.*

I walked into the living room, sat down on the couch and gave myself permission—allowed the emotion to finally have its way. He was no longer connected to me as he had been for a lifetime. The feelings of hollowness and isolation—a concentrated body experience beyond grief and death. It was over. I felt pain and loss everywhere.

Tears. I made no attempt to stop them or ease the wrenching convulsions of my body. Purged were the toxins of a past life. This was for closure, completion of the process.

I have only a sense of what those moments were like, nothing more, as experiences need safe trauma-free time to gel before they can become fixed memories. I was in that nongelled place. My experiences would *never* become memories. I was glad.

It seemed appropriate for me to be alone. No distractions. No discounting the end. Nothing to stop me from honoring the reality of the *get*. I had to remain with the excruciating sensations and ride out the loss until the ache became distant. The harsh feelings cemented the disconnection, allowing the experience of being completely alone to become real. Unattached and alone. Such a virgin concept.

Having someone around to diminish the pain or fill the void was a powerful attraction. Despite the fear of loneliness, a new life with another could not be imagined.

> Not ready
> to share toothpaste
> fragile
> vulnerable.
> Not ready
> for *anyone* to
> join
> this brittle existence.

This roller coaster in the Outer Limits had no simple loops or curves. I didn't know where the ride was going or when it would end. It frightened me to be in this jarred grieflike state. Often I felt the sadness would never leave.

Many who were well-intentioned suggested that enough time had passed that I should *get on with my life.* But I knew this process had a timetable of its own. Most people simply did not have the necessary tolerance to be empathetic. I learned quickly when asked "How are you?" to respond "Fine." I was uncomfortable with the dishonesty, but people did not want to hear what it was *really* like.

I remained with the emotions as they surfaced. And I reached out to those who loved me—my daughter, my sister, good friends and family. Thankfully, they recognized my need for distance as well as nurturing.

A tough balancing act was acknowledging and experiencing the grief while avoiding the attraction of its blackness. I needed to remember the ultimate goal: Move beyond the sadness.

Slowly the intensity of emotions began to diminish. I developed awareness of movement forward and backward along a continuum of healing. I stayed away from romantic movies. Learned my lesson from *Sleepless in Seattle,* as I silently screamed, *I know about magic in a relationship!*

I surrounded myself with cheerful experiences and possessions. I placed an old-fashioned candy jar in the kitchen, bought Daffy Duck coffee mugs and left around upbeat notes from my daughter. My eye would catch a note: "Hi, Mom. Am working out. Have a great day. Love you." And for a moment I would forget that she was 2,000 miles away. Having the notes around was like having her home. Then I didn't miss her as much.

The question I asked was always the same. Is this going to help me move beyond the sadness? The depth of my grief frightened me, and I was willing to go to great lengths in order simply to smile again.

I understood the power of laughter in healing. *Mr. Blanding Builds His Dreamhouse* and *Sleeper* were regular viewing experiences. Laughter improved my moods and gave my immune system a boost. I didn't care if I was tricking my body and mind. Survival was the goal.

I came to tolerate my alone experience, as I understood that no one could do the emotional work for me. The intensity of feelings served a specific purpose. This was my emotional road map. I needed to pay attention to the guideposts and journey beyond the tethers of sadness.

I like to use the word "transcender" in relation to trauma. Such a great word filled with optimism. I began to believe that I could transcend the loss by letting go of those restraining negative thoughts and emotions. I simply needed to allow the *get* to do its work.

I heard Alice Walker talk about the need to "honor the difficult." I loved those words that implied acceptance as opposed to struggle. It is easier to work beyond and through from a place of acceptance—the old quicksand metaphor.

I promised myself not to stay stuck or dwell on what was lost. It was important for me to accept in order to move beyond.

Now was the time for a paradigm shift. Time to focus on what I had in my life instead of what I had lost. It sounded so simple, and it felt so good.

22

Walking Taller

Photos of a past life had covered the walls of *Bellaire*—pictures that had become part of my existence and history. Special family pictures that could not be displayed again.

In many ways, it is easier when someone dies. At least the photographs can remain on the wall.

In the new house I hung old pictures of my daughter and her father. I believed those pictures acknowledged his

existence in her life and represented a continuity that she
ached for. But pictures of the three of us, like the Copper
Mountain ski photo—well, those were banished. I missed
their presence and the life they represented.

One special missing photographic essay hung in a huge
frame that blended old black-and-white photographs of me
and the man who had shared my bed. Restored pictures of
us as little kids, on bicycles and ponies and on docks at
lakes—with our fathers and our mothers.

This huge collage had hung prominently on its own wall
at *Bellaire*. Its life force pulsated, as simply passing by created a physical, almost seductive experience. The haunting
pictures reached out and grabbed. Sometimes I would just
lose myself in one specific photograph, becoming engulfed
by its history and presence.

During the separation and several subsequent moves, the
special collage had been relegated to permanent basement
status. This was one picture I didn't think I could ever hang
again. Those powerful images could not be faced on a daily
basis. The large frame, covered with brown wrapping paper
from distant moves, remained untouched until I was visited
by a young friend.

"What happened to the collage?" she asked.

Her simple question caused me to rethink how getting on with life after divorce creates an unbalanced thought process. The clouded desire is to start fresh, toss out the old hurtful memories. But what is forgotten or not realized is that the good memories are also trashed in the process. It's like chemotherapy. The toxins kill the good cells along with the bad—not much discrimination in the process.

I saw myself making this mistake as I realized how much I missed certain comforting possessions from my past life. This was—possibly—an unnecessary loss, one that could be avoided. I thought about the huge frame, which I never intended to hang in the new home—the memories of when it last had a life were just too hurtful.

For three years I collected and arranged old black-and-white photographs of the two of us. It was an optimistic period for our family. As I carefully chose each picture for the collage, I imagined this frame would hang in our house forever. This was definitely a labor of love—a testament to our union and the future of our life together. Our grandchildren would ask us questions. "Grandma, Grandpa, who's that a picture of?"

With heart pounding, I journeyed downstairs and vaulted into my basement past. Ripped off the brown protective paper only to face the images I missed and feared. I would experiment, hang the collage and see how it felt. If I could find the right spot, a wall of its own—well, maybe it could stay.

The experience of hanging that huge picture from my past represented so much more than positioning a collage on a wall. First of all, bringing it up from the basement, one stair at a time, doing it myself—that was a physical triumph.

I didn't think I could hang it myself. The picture was too heavy to lift. But I became very creative. And getting the picture on the wall, by myself, became a powerful metaphor. I was determined.

After it was up, I stood close, gazing at those neglected absent images. I reached out and touched them individually, one picture at a time. As the tears dried, a profound sense of calm and completion overwhelmed me. I knew the right decision had been made.

The man who had been my spouse remarried four months after the *get*. Oddly enough, he did not marry my friend. He ended that relationship and became attached quickly to a new woman he would call wife, an Orthodox woman I did not know. Now he could enjoy the traditional life he desired.

I concluded that his satisfaction with life was good. From a completely selfish perspective, his happiness was best for our daughter. It didn't make any sense for me to wish misery on the father of the daughter I loved. His sadness would then become her sadness, as parents hand their emotions to their children, like gifts neatly wrapped.

I was actually pleased for him and hoped that I was being honest about not feeling resentful or sad. I was comfortable with his new marriage and believed we could be friends. I even bought them a wedding present. The surgery had been successful.

Life was very different after the *get*. Occasionally I experienced a sense of exhilaration, in many ways reminiscent of the sixties. I experimented with my new existence. Let the house stay messy for weeks at a time. I actually left dishes in the sink. For me that was hard, considering my compulsive nature. I found pleasure in food again, even though sometimes my dinner consisted of only corn on the cob.

I felt like a little kid getting the Happy Meal at McDonald's. After all those years of cooking regular dinners most nights, sitting down to four ears of corn and nothing else felt so liberating.

The exhilaration that accompanied eating only what I wanted, when I wanted, surprised me. Some nights I skipped dinner completely and sat down late—with ice cream, caramel sauce, chocolate morsels, whipped cream and a beer. What joy, and how simple.

I don't think women realize how we put our desires last. I never thought about what I wanted for dinner. It was always what others wanted. This selflessness becomes the way we live within our families. It doesn't feel self-sacrificing or like martyrdom; it just becomes the way things are done. And women become so programmed to function as caretakers that it actually feels good to let others' desires come first. All of the time.

This new sense of freedom was not limited to food choices or mealtimes. It went beyond staying up reading in bed until 3:00 in the morning. More than joining a women's poker group or seeing friends for dinner without having to call home. Not needing to explain daily experiences was so adult.

I worked to become accustomed to the singleness of my daily life. For the first time, I did not have to tell anyone that I would be home late. Nothing profound here, but to me it felt earth-shattering.

I came to realize how much of my existence was programmed to think of others first. Such a contrary existence, this not being accountable to anyone in my personal life. It was like there was a new kid on the block that I had to introduce myself to and get to know.

Such a sense of freedom. It was luscious. I had to fight the feelings of guilt. It seemed so wrong to be living my life this way.

The pain lessened its grip as I gained emotional strength. I walked taller, felt lighter and was sad less often. I actually began to feel happy, an emotion I wasn't sure I could ever feel again. And I continued to be drawn toward anything that held the slightest promise of healing and emotional growth.

23

Kaddish

Emotional support is received after the death of a spouse. But when one experiences divorce, this same compassion is nonexistent. Divorce trauma is viewed as a less significant loss. In many ways it is discounted and can be viewed as a stigma. According to Jewish law, there were now some men *(Kohanim)* who were not allowed to marry me because of my divorced status.

The irony is, I truly believe, that divorce can be a far more difficult trauma to work through emotionally. On the surface it looks as though it would hurt a lot less than death, but it actually feels much worse. The experience is similar to being a survivor who escapes unharmed from a horrible car wreck. Working through this trauma is often more difficult than if there had been severe physical injuries. The absence of marks or wounds causes others to discount the survivor's emotional pain, and therefore less support is expected. Friends will say, "Boy, are you lucky. You weren't even hurt."

In my reality, the lack of support seemed to accentuate the pain. I felt guilty that I still experienced sadness and had difficulty connecting to the real world. *What more did I have to do in order to feel normal again?*

The Kaddish is a potent Aramaic prayer that has become synonymous with death and mourning. After a significant loss, one is obligated to recite the Kaddish for a specific period of time, depending on who is being mourned.

Several versions of Kaddish are recited during services, and a special Kaddish is said at graveside. The Kaddish that is said near the end of religious services has become known as the Mourner's Kaddish.

This association with death and mourning is interesting since there is no mention of either in the prayer. Kaddish

actually validates the meaning of life and honors the great-
ness of God. By reciting the prayer, one publicly affirms
one's belief and faith. Rising in the congregation to say
Kaddish is an uplifting experience about hope and possibilities, not sadness and loss.

I knew that saying Kaddish had tremendous therapeutic
value. The chanting of the Aramaic—the various rhythms—
seems to create a physical and emotional response. It is a
powerful experience.

Because this intense loss felt so much like a physical
death, saying Kaddish made sense to me when a friend suggested it. My experience held all of the trappings of a death.
Just the body was missing. It was possible that saying
Kaddish could be another necessary component in
acknowledging the death of my relationship—and its finality. In addition to being therapeutic, reciting the prayer
would be a tribute to the memory of my marriage and also
a formal honoring of its end. I decided to chant the Kaddish
on the first Shabbat after the *get*.

This was not my first experience reciting Kaddish. I said
the prayer for my parents and for relatives and special

friends I had lost over the years. I was quite familiar with the powerfully emotive sound of the words.

In the past, when it came time to say the prayer at the end of services, I would stand calmly, with eyes closed. The recitation of Kaddish came freely and easily to my mind. It became a meditation. Looking at the prayer book was no longer necessary—the words were imprinted on my soul.

No one at my *havurah* knew I was going to recite Kaddish for the death of my marriage. This was an exceptionally private experience and a fairly radical concept that I came to believe was integral to my healing.

As the time approached for mourners to rise, I became extremely anxious. It almost felt like panic. I had prepared myself for the moment to be emotionally difficult, but I had not expected that I would be unable to stand.

The room circled my head as the walls began to close in. With the excess noise in my head, I wasn't sure the words would come out correctly, or if I would hear when it was the appropriate time to stand. *Had I missed the prayer? Maybe I should just wait until next week when I felt better.*

I heard, "Will those in mourning please rise?" My heart

pounded. Could people sitting near me hear? I began to drip as I became flushed with heat. My breathing was shallow and rapid. I felt light-headed. As I rose and thought about the meaning of this powerful gesture, I was not so sure that my legs would support me. It felt like the *get* all over again. How could this be? I thought I was *done*. I began.

> *Yeet ga-dal*
> *ve-yeet ka-dash*
> *sh-may ra-ba.*

My heart throbbed in my throat as I stood not so firmly. An unsteady voice cracked in the midst of the emotionally potent prayer. I began to cry.

I know I did not chant all of the words as I experienced another realm somewhere outside of myself. The feelings were profound as I remained deceptively calm. I made it to the end of the prayer and sat down quietly. Overwhelmed with silent grief, no one noticed as I said good-bye again.

It amazed me how many times I felt that I was past the pain, only to have more feelings surface. This was the dry heaves, vomiting when nothing remained in the stomach. Or dusting furniture in the sunlight. Moments later another layer appeared.

I recited Kaddish for eleven months. With each week the sadness decreased, and the emotions became less intense. The ancient Aramaic contained a potency that honored and healed at the same time. It also created a pointedness—brought me back to the here and now. It became a continued reminder of the death of my marriage and validation in the power of something outside my skin. It was not morbid. It was enlightening.

By returning to my *havurah* to recite the Kaddish, I reconnected with those special people I had missed. My spiritual ties deepened, as did my feelings of gratitude for all that was good in my life. I paid attention to those who were my friends as I came to learn of the truly important people in my life. I accepted the ones who still could not look me in the eye. I understood their fear.

People who have limbs amputated experience the feeling that the missing limbs are still part of their bodies. Even though those limbs have been physically severed, they have body sensations that give them the odd feeling that the limbs are still attached.

The loss of my marriage felt like a phantom limb. Even though the *get* had done its work, just like an amputation, old sensations remained. Despite the realness of my ended marriage, at times I still felt married. Changing a thirty-year pattern took time. As I said often in my office, "The head knows, but sometimes the heart doesn't."

24

Sidetracked

Last holiday season was bad. It felt really empty, and the extreme sadness concerned me. I spiraled downward without emotional control, feeling sorry for myself as I got caught up in the missing-my-former-life syndrome. The focus again was on everything I had lost. My envious eyes caught happy couples everywhere, preparing for *their* ten days in Vail.

I found myself consumed with thoughts of friends I used to be with, celebrations I went to, a mountain house I called home and the marriage that took care of me. My list of things I had lost was pretty long. I kept sinking lower and lower, as I noticed only the other people I believed to be happy.

"Sidetracked"—I heard quarterback John Elway use that word when he spoke about the difficulty of staying focused while surrounded by Super Bowl media hoopla.

"You can get sidetracked real easy," he had said.

I guess that's what happened to me.

My focus was no longer on gratitude as I allowed myself to be sucked into fearful negative thoughts. Getting sidetracked was a nice way of putting it. I let the dark side slip in.

It amazed me how I periodically could become brain dead—sleepwalking through daily experiences. I simply forgot the essentials. Remain focused. Always pay attention. "Keep your awareness on your unawareness," as my friend Stanley used to say.

I came to see fear and negativity as directional points on the compass of life. Little gifts that could guide us *away* from the dark—toward the good, healthy experiences that can be ours.

I silently battled my newly assigned role. In my *havurah,* where family defined one's existence, I was now a single Jewish female. *Havdalah* and retreats were exceptionally difficult—a constant reminder of the life I used to have.

I realized that my spiritual life felt less genuine—something I allowed to happen when my thinking patterns became just another manifestation of me feeling sorry for me. My thinking centered on how alone I felt during services, instead of how special the services were. It's all about focus. Gratitude. The right thoughts.

One cannot simultaneously be spiritual and have self-defeating thoughts. Whenever negative thoughts occur, any possibility of connecting with God at that moment is shattered. One simply cannot be negative and spiritual at the same time.

I had to regain my spiritual connection and live the life that God wanted me to live. There really was no choice here. Deep down I knew that the power, the source, the light, the force—whatever name you assigned—had intended for me to be an agent for good. Before this was possible, I first had to be good to myself. I had to end self-defeating thoughts. It was time to stop beating myself up with sadness.

I don't exactly know what turned my thoughts around. Possibly it was the realization that I had been influenced by the dialog raging in my head. Nothing had been altered outside my skin. It was my thinking that had changed. Those not-good perceptions of self had taken over.

By feeling sorry for myself, I stayed stuck. The poor-me syndrome accentuated my situation and kept me in a negative, fearful state. Had good things come my way, I probably would have missed them. Like finding a hundred-dollar bill on the street, but telling myself that it probably was counterfeit. I needed to shift my focus in order to ameliorate my thoughts. And, most important, not only did thinking need to be altered, *behaviors* had to significantly change, too.

This wasn't simply a matter of enhanced positive thinking. I had to actively concentrate on the abundant elements in my life. Joy and laughter needed to return. Not exactly breaking news. Sleepwalking again. I wasn't being very smart. I knew this stuff.

Insight is critical to change but pretty useless without parallel changes in behavior. That's why folks can experience years of therapy without getting any better. Charlie Brown was never going to kick the football successfully unless he experienced major behavior changes, and Charles Schultz was not going to allow that to happen. "That wouldn't be Charlie Brown," Schultz said, acknowledging that his famous cartoon character was never going to do things differently.

Most folks believe that altering behavior is impossible, that we are like puppets on the string of life. But I believe that change is always possible—always an option—a conscious choice. But the most critical pieces—thinking *and*

behavior—must be transformed in order to improve one's life condition. It is this difficult transformation that creates meaningful, persistent change.

If my life is run by fear and denial, it doesn't matter how many self-help books I read or how long I am in therapy. Nothing will change until I *decide* to change. And the decision to change is not possible unless I view the world differently. I had to envision the world as a good place.

I made a conscious decision to improve my life. I began to watch funny feel-good movies again—my antidote to a lowered immune system, above and below the neck. The Three Stooges, Abbott and Costello, the Marx Brothers, *You Can't Take It with You* and, of course, *The Producers.* In addition, I made lists. Gratitude lists. Lists of goals. This was a paradigm shift.

The most significant change was that I *committed* to accomplishing these goals. For the first time, I made a simple but difficult promise to myself. *I would follow through and keep my commitments.*

The internal chatter intruded again saying, *Helloooo. . . . You've never done this before. This is really new. You've*

committed to things in the past, but you've never made a binding
promise to yourself to really follow through. . . . Like if someone held a gun to my head.

I recalled a radio interview I had heard years earlier. A
domestic violence counselor who worked with abusive
males talked about getting these men to change their
behavior. Hitting could never be an option. He said, "I ask
these men what they would do if I put a gun to their heads
and promised to pull the trigger the moment they hit their
wives. Their response was always the same. 'Well, I guess I
wouldn't ever hit my wife.'"

I needed to put a psychological gun to my head. There
could be no escape route. This was for getting beyond survival. I was tired of being sucked back down into the hole,
slowly working my way out, only to be sucked back down
again. There must be an end to the seductive negative cycle
that held me back.

I had to pay better attention to the dark side and all its
insidious forms, like procrastination—that shredder of self-
esteem. Procrastination continually re-creates a black

self-destructive thought cycle. Procrastination is truly a slow killer of self.

The really scary piece for me was finding a three-year-old to-do list that could have been written that day. My current list was identical. *Clean out the garage. Get my body in shape. Increase my net worth. Read* Huckleberry Finn. *Get on top of my paperwork. Organize my files.*

It was embarrassing. The list had not changed in three years. I wasn't even able to scratch off Mark Twain's masterpiece. I asked myself if the list would be the same in ten years—and how would I feel about myself then.

> I had to make a committed decision
> to end
> procrastination.

25

Garage Sale

I parked my car on the street because I couldn't get into the garage. It was filled with stuff. Floor to ceiling. Things. Nice things that I had planned on selling.

Systematically I added more to the already bursting garage, in a quest to simplify and free myself of burdensome things. I know it sounds contradictory, but it made sense at the time, even though my garage was now becoming unmanageable.

The process of freeing myself of stuff was not easy. Everything seemed difficult to discard. But before anything was relegated to the garage, I first engaged in an endless argument with myself.

> *Haven't worn this in three years.*
> *What makes me think I will wear it this year?*
> *But it was such a costly suit.*
> *When are you going to wear it?*
> *I don't know.*
> *Get rid of it now.*
> *But it's almost brand new.*
> *Okay.*

Or I could hear my daughter: "Mo-om! No. Not my orange Bronco turtleneck."

Life was becoming simpler, and it actually looked like I was getting something accomplished. The house emptied of unused stuff as the garage filled. Once an item reached the garage, I experienced a feeling of completion. Finality. A decision had been made.

Soon I would be ready to post my signs: "Garage Sale This Sunday." I even bought a book, *The Complete Garage Sale Kit: Everything You Need to Make Money at Your Next*

Garage Sale! It came with ready-to-copy signs for posting and hints on advertising. The book was very helpful, but just the thought of preparing for the event propelled me into overwhelm.

The merchandise inside the garage grew with each week that passed. I now had eight large, tightly filled clothes racks. People would drive by.

"Stuff looks great. When's the sale?"

So much more was continually added to the garage that a path ceased to exist. Moving through this museum of unwanted history became difficult. When I ran out of floor space I hung stuff on the walls. Soon the walls were covered. All three. Covered with baseball caps, backpacks, sports equipment, artwork—life's things.

Any passing thought about the garage gave me that uncomfortable feeling in my stomach. It became a source of embarrassment. No matter how good I began to feel about myself, because of accomplishments in other areas of my life, that overstuffed garage—the procrastination—represented a failure.

Such an unimportant thing
that kept me
stuck
shredded my sense of self
strangled my
productivity and created
overwhelm.

I promised myself that the garage sale would become a reality. But instead it progressively became a self-defeating dark cloud that hampered any movement forward. My garage, that abyss of things, continued to be a nagging reminder of something I wanted to get done but, for some reason, just was not able to accomplish.

Whenever I had a free moment I could be found in the garage. Getting ready. Yet each day that passed without completion became another day for me to kick myself. Neighbors began to tease me. My garage became a joke as I entered the second year of organization. I definitely was losing credibility.

"Be sure to tell me when you're having your sale," a neighbor would say, with an expression of disbelief.

One Sunday morning, after many more months had slipped by, I admitted to myself the possibility that I might never be ready for the garage sale. It was that *perfectionism* piece: the perfect garage sale.

The goal of organizing the garage was to make items more attractive and easy to sell. I had summer clothes on one rack, dress clothes on another. One rack was filled with jackets, one with sweaters. It looked like a store. And of course, I couldn't sell anything that wasn't clean, so I washed and ironed most of the clothes. I wanted them to look new.

Almost everything in the garage was of high quality, and because of this I planned on asking top dollar for my clothes. I had telephones, new office supplies and an HP printer in perfect working condition. Stuff. So much great stuff.

Friends told me that garage sales didn't work like that. People were not interested in paying good prices for garage sale items, no matter how nice they were. But I wouldn't listen.

Perfectionism and procrastination go hand in hand. They feed on each other. Nothing gets finished until it is done perfectly. The end result is that nothing gets accomplished. Except one does get to feel bad about getting nothing done. It is called "secondary gain." Then of course the source of perfectionism and procrastination is always fear, which stops us dead in our tracks.

The previous November I actually had an ad in the paper. The weekend was all set, but then I had to leave town unexpectedly and the sale had to be canceled. When I returned home, I told myself that I would have the sale after football season.

No one in Denver would have a Sunday garage sale during the fall, and I couldn't have it on Saturday because that was Shabbat. Thirteen months later, the Broncos were in the playoffs and I was looking at a January date. January? Who has a garage sale in the middle of winter? Can you see the dilemma and why I was feeling bad about myself as the holiday season approached?

When I realized that the garage sale was not going to happen until spring, I felt overwhelming shame. That's when I made the decision to give it all away. And that's when I understood what was *really* holding me back.

Completion. I became exhilarated by the thought. It seemed so simple. I wondered why I had not seen the solution before. Possibly it was the money issue. These things were too good to give away. What an unkind thought. Especially as we approached the winter holiday season of giving.

My first impulse was to call an organization and have the stuff all hauled away. It could have been gone in a few hours. Simple. Instead, I decided that it was important for me to find an organization that would give my special possessions directly to people. I thought of a shelter where women had nothing except the clothes they were wearing. These women needed appropriate clothing to wear to job interviews. I had a garage filled with such clothes.

I promised myself that this was not just more procrastination in order to find the perfect recipient, even though it might appear that way. I knew that it would have been much easier to simply call and have everything hauled away. But those charities that picked up donations also had stores.

I wanted my things to go directly to people who could use them. And I didn't want some of my possessions to wind up in a garbage dump because someone was too lazy to inventory them. Sometimes that happened. So I began to call shelters and leave messages. Lots of messages.

"I have a whole bunch of really nice things that I want to give away. Could you please get back to me?"

I must say I was surprised when no one called me back. Rarely did I ever get past an annoying voice-mail message. "Please listen carefully as our menu options have changed."

When I actually succeeded in getting a real person on the telephone, I was told something like "Our shelter is just too filled with donations. You'll have to wait until after the holidays. Don't you know that *everyone* wants to give us stuff at this time of year. You know—for taxes."

Several organizations' recorded messages stated the specific hours and days when they would accept items. And of course there were the exclusive shelters, with their messages that said, "We only accept items in perfect condition." I began to wonder and I got angry. "I can't even *give* this shit away. Why is it so hard?"

I hoped that I was not sabotaging my efforts to free myself of clutter. Or that I was not making this project more difficult than necessary. I kept on telling myself all I wanted was to find an agency that would be happy to get my stuff. A place that might say, "These things are really nice—thanks."

One day I found the right place—the Volunteers of America shelter in Denver. No menu options at the switchboard. Real people answering the telephone. No arrogance or rudeness like so many of the other organizations. No one made me feel like they were doing me a favor. They actually apologized for not having a truck, and they sounded so excited. They said that they always needed clothes and household items, and if the things were nice, then that was really appreciated. I could bring the donations just about anytime during the day. And most important, my things were given directly to people. No store.

Whenever I had time, I filled up my black Jetta and took down a carload. One load at a time. It was an immense project.

If I would have had any sense at all, I might have realized why it took me so long to deal with my stuff. And why it also would have been a mistake to let a truck haul it away in one afternoon.

Just another significant life transition—that's all. *Cleaning out my garage* as metaphor. This lengthy bizarre process of giving away stuff came to represent the sum total of my life—the past, the present and the future possibilities.

I loaded my car many times when the items became mixed with the salt of tears. Our first set of silverware. Our first set of dishes. The hopes and dreams imagined as we carefully picked out the pattern. A lamp we bought from Hal Lipstein and a painting that hung in our first apartment at the Logan House. Did I envision this cold garage as two lovers purchased a piece of art for their life together?

Why did I still have these things? What encouraged me to hold on to a rose tile from the *Bellaire* kitchen? And why was I crying? Again. Yes I had visions of forever when the remodel was completed. This was the kitchen my grandchildren would come to for cookies—and chicken soup.

How could the emotions still be present? I had worked so hard to be free from those memories and the sadness. It can't still hurt. Obviously, not all of the venom had been sucked out.

I was amazed at how good I felt the moment the decision was made to give everything away. The folks at the shelter were so happy and so thankful, I wanted to empty my whole house. It seemed like I did.

Lighter. Happier immediately. I had not realized what an emotional burden that filled garage was. A dark space stuffed with memories of a past life. Memories I did not have the strength to deal with, until now.

This simple yet difficult Zen act of adding to and emptying my garage snowballed into positive feelings and raised self-esteem. Catharsis. I got to pat myself on the back, instead of kick myself in the rear.

With each transitional carload I felt better. I came to understand why I had taken this difficult route of sorting and delivering the items myself. This residual marital property had tethers I was forced to cut away. My fear piece.

I came to see how significant a problem procrastination was—representative of something far deeper than simply not getting things done. There was always a reason. Most often, it was fear.

I felt dissonance within, as I came to see that I never actually *decided* to get anything done. I was just great at making lists. I understood the emotional significance of this and the role that it played in my continuing sadness.

I choose
to make commitments
to myself
and
to honor those commitments
I screamed from a high place.

I still made lists but now with a new sense of purpose. I came to finally understand, in a profound way, that goals were meaningless without a distinct behavior change and a promise to oneself to follow through.

The feelings overwhelmed, but in a positive way. I had discovered a recipe for moving beyond the logjam of procrastination, perfection and fear. Most likely there were more "garages" in my life that I needed to move beyond, but right now I felt content. At last I came to know—in an intensely personal way—the power of commitment and freeing oneself from stuff. It was like an elixir.

26

Frugality and Beyond

Financial planners seem to often prepare women for the loss of a husband through death—but not divorce. Two very different economic realities. I never thought about either.

I had not planned for my marriage to end. When it did, I had no savings for attorney fees or college tuition. The divorce generated a tremendous amount of debt, and I was forced to borrow money for the first time in my life.

The money I owed became oppressive. It sapped my energy and creativity. I played a shell game each month and paid my bills with apprehension and reluctance. This was wrong. Paying what one owes is an honoring of the universe.

I struggled against a poverty mentality, the thought process of people who are not poor but believe they are. These folks see themselves as victims, always letting others pick up the check, never being generous. They clip coupons, only make purchases on sale and would never buy anything at Tiffany's, even though they could afford it. Their every action in life becomes guided by this mentality of not having enough.

The way we perceive the world often becomes a self-fulfilling prophecy. Tendencies to be cheap keep us stuck in a negative thought process that defines what we believe we-do-not-have. Our head holds us back financially (not our circumstances) as we become victims of these beliefs. The limits of our finances—held hostage by our very own thoughts.

My life had changed drastically as a result of the divorce, and much of what I accepted as part of everyday existence now became a luxury I could not afford. The divorce debt threw me into a frugal lifestyle, and I began to feel poor.

I did not realize that this new existence caused me to focus, again, on how very much I did not have. Without awareness I had spiraled into that which I had feared—a poverty mentality—and it came to affect my entire sense of self.

I thought of that great scene in the very beginning of *Schindler's List*. Schindler, although he appears almost penniless, thrusts his energy into acting the part of an influential moneyed gentleman. He dresses, spends and projects, as though he has money and power. Soon he does.

I decided not to let fear enter my consciousness in the form of money concerns. Fear would simply give life to the thoughts, and possibly act as a magnet attracting its object. I had to act like I had money, in the face of my financial reality. A tough balancing act.

I fought viewing the world through a lens of scarcity. I just refused to do so. This money situation was simply a transition to better things. My daughter reminded me often, "Mom, we are not poor. We have so much to be thankful for."

Instead of feeling deprived because I was cutting out so much, I began to focus on my internal wealth—my *abundance*. I felt an immediate surge of control over my life. It was like the wealth I felt on Shabbat when I didn't drive or watch TV or shop in stores.

I devoured any author that pointed me toward strength of self—Stephen Covey, Tony Robbins, Emmet Fox, John Templeton, Abraham Twerski and many others. And thank you, Suze Orman, for helping me to understand the importance of changing my money reality. I wanted the courage to have a prosperous life, but I knew that first I had to believe, change behavior and think of my life in terms of abundance.

I again gave money to charity, even though it was a small amount. I looked forward to paying my bills each month— viewing the process with gratitude. I took friends to lunch. I began to write affirmations about huge amounts of money coming into my life. I talked about becoming a philanthropist. Silly I know, but why not? I think what Bill Gates does is wonderful.

By taking these proactive steps I began to feel in control of my financial existence. I experienced gratitude and felt as though I now had choices in my life. I could breathe again.

27

Use It or Lose It

I used to work out at the Cherry Creek Sporting Club. During the separation, I allowed my membership to lapse. My entire exercise regimen came to a halt as I found excuses for not working out. Getting in shape could be found at the top of many to-do lists. Neglect of my body was just another piece of the overwhelm package and the negative self-talk. Divorce residue. You can imagine how the dialogue went: *No time. I don't even have a club to go to. I can't run anymore.*

My intellect knew the importance of physical activity— not just for my body but for my head. It was all part of the negative spiral downward. "When you're in the box, you're in the box," Jack used to say. But now that I was making changes and breakthroughs, a way out seemed possible.

I promised myself to check off goals on my list, and getting strong physically was definitely on the list. It was time to stop making excuses, because in the scheme of life there *were* no excuses—only choices. If I didn't take charge of my body now, it was going to turn on me, as I stared closely at my golden years. I believed passionately in "use it or lose it."

I loved to run. As a kid I was always the fastest, but in those days girls weren't encouraged in that way. At Lakeview High School, gym, as it was called, was pretty much of a humiliation. Green gym suits and standing in formations. We were graded according to the crisp pleats in our uniforms.

I didn't rediscover my love of running until the early seventies when I decided to be good to my body. I remember going into a store looking for a woman's running shoe. The store had only one pair in my size, with a sole that looked like a sheet of colored construction paper. We've come a long way.

Running for me was a passion. I understood that line in *Chariots of Fire* about running and feeling God's pleasure. I felt connected to *Hashem* (Hasidic name for God) during my morning run.

When I became pregnant, my doctor told me that I could continue to run as long as my body approved. I ran into my ninth month. And after I had my precious one, using a stroller, I pushed her around the track at George Washington High School. Women weren't doing that in those days and people stared.

Several years later I was training for a marathon, when I did a stupid thing. I became seduced by an undulating con-crete bike path. As I moved out of normal consciousness on my early morning run, I formed a connection with the smooth curves of the new pavement. I was unaware of the threat to my body. Concrete is sometimes unforgiving.

One day the pain hit suddenly at seven miles out. Instead of doing the smart thing—walking back—I ran home because of time. Two days later the pain hit at four miles out. The next time at two miles out. The last time I ran, I couldn't make a mile without intense pain in my hip. This was not transitional pain. I could not run beyond it.

I went to doctors all over the city. No one could tell me what caused the pain. One doctor said that it might be arthritis, one said possibly bursitis. Everyone told me to stop running. Which I did.

Most exercises that I attempted as a replacement had similar hip action and caused the same pain, like rowing, biking and step classes. I even tried walking. Extremely frustrated, I stopped working out. Completely.

Every once in a while, with the belief that the injury had healed, I would enthusiastically go out for a run. But the pain would strike at a half mile. Once the pain began, I could not even walk through it. I came to accept that I would never be able to run again. That was ten years ago.

Now, with a new commitment and a different awareness, I decided to see if I could begin to run again. My daughter bought me an aerobic video, and I purchased some free weights. I placed all of my energy into believing that it was possible to run again. I was determined to find a way. Even if I could only run two or three miles, I would be satisfied.

I realized that after my injury I had simply accepted the inability to run without pain. With professional verification, it became a given, a reality that I believed to be true. Now, with my perspective altered, I approached running with new optimism. I refused to accept that running pain-free was not possible. I decided to be smart this time, as I created a new running reality.

My workout video had a strong stretching component, something I had never done much of before. Lifting free weights was also new. I sensed that my body was changing.

I heard about a foot doctor who seemed to be helping runners get through injuries. I decided to make an appointment with Dr. Griffin to see if he could help me to run again.

Griffin puts you through an incredible evaluative process. He casts your foot for orthotics and then video-tapes you running in shoes, without socks, on a treadmill. He is looking for stability and the relationship between the foot, ankle, knee and hip. When the process is complete, he hands you the orthotics and tells you which running shoes to buy. It's all very scientific, and it usually works.

With state-of-the-art running shoes and my orthotics in place, I was ready to begin. My goal was to run three miles with my daughter in Maine when I visited her for Parents' Weekend.

I began with a quarter-mile run and a quarter-mile walk, three to four days a week. I *slowly* increased my distance. I did my video workout at least twice a week. After each exercise regimen, I stretched vigorously. I ended each run with at least ten minutes of walking and a feeling of gratitude, as each morning I thanked *Hashem* for the ability to run again.

Many months later during Parents' Weekend in Brunswick, Maine, my daughter and I had an incredible run. Up and down magnificent glistening country roads in the midst of crisp air and pungent smells, we ran three miles and walked three miles. Fall is such a high time anyway, but this was one of those days when the endorphins kicked in and the body simply did not want to stop. It was like running through a postcard as we danced among the sharp reds and yellows. Something was very different.

No awareness of
feet touching the
road.
No awareness of two
people.
Only one singular
stride.

I was so blessed for this moment in cosmic time. I recall thinking to myself,

If this was all there ever was to be
it would be more than enough.

At my side. The precious infant I pushed around the track when dreams of family were so vivid. The grown child that I now caused so much pain. Did she know how regretful I was?

I am sorry for this wound
I handed to you so neatly wrapped.

No words passed between us to distract.

28

Slow Learner

I decided to stop chasing the people who, I finally had to admit, were no longer interested in my friendship. I came to accept that most couples who had been good friends for over twenty years were not going to invite me to dinner parties and holiday celebrations. *This* was the most difficult acknowledgment, and so hard to understand. But it was time to let them go.

The people who wanted to be in my life made sure that they had a presence. They would call with invitations. They would check on me. Their continued support and love became an immeasurable life-sustaining force.

I came to accept one crucial, inexorable belief. My life had to be a *continuous* process of change and development. I had to grow intellectually, physically, emotionally and spiritually. I learned that if I neglected any one of those areas my entire existence suffered—immediately.

I know this sounds strange, but it began to feel as though the Jewish holy days were scripted by therapists. After all, those special times were really about change, rattling one's comfortable existence, doing it better next time, becoming emotionally free. The spiritual work originated from a place of gratitude and created clarity of purpose. This became the foundation of my existence. I understood how important it was to push the envelope on my comforts—to live outside the box.

We are constantly given the opportunity to improve ourselves—to be our very best. The path is laid out for us. There is definitely a specific blueprint. We simply have to follow it.

I know by now you're thinking that I'm a pretty slow learner. Probably so. But this *was* repetition of the trauma. Freud did have a lot of it right. There *is* a compulsion to do all of this traumatic stuff over.

The turning toward strength coincided with the decision to let go and give away my *stuff.* The vulnerability I experienced sensitized me to the opportunitites I simply had not been able to see. I realized how closed I had become—how relaxed in my zone of comfort. I felt increased potential now. It almost felt manic. Good things began to happen. I came to fiercely believe in endless possibilities. The odd part was that I never felt I stopped having faith. But clearly I had. Divorce clouds perceptions of self—it is such a pervasive wound.

I began to study Kabbalah, arranged to do a Fisher Divorce Seminar and completed the Landmark Forum. I made time to read more books. I felt proactive. In charge. In control. I created good things in my life as I finally achieved the clarity and freedom to move forward.

Fear became the next challenge, as I knew that specific fears held me captive. Kept me stuck. Caused me to limit the possibilities. Along with procrastination, fear is another slow killer of self-esteem. You can't be afraid and feel good about yourself at the same time.

It made sense that I could offer my world so much more if I conquered my own fears first. It takes confidence and a strong sense of self to be a good therapist. How could I impart these qualities to my patients if I did not possess them myself?

Of course. My special AA friend Jack once told me, "Therapy is as high as the therapist." I don't think I understood what he meant then, but I do now.

The silly thing about fear is that it really is like a magnet. Whatever you become afraid of, you seem to attract. I wish I would have kept count of every time a patient walked into my office saying, "You won't believe this, but my worst fear came true." Whether it was the person who lived in fear of being rear-ended in a car accident, or the mother who feared her daughter would be abused. People seem, sadly, to get what they fear.

Think about what we might have attracted. *I'm afraid that I won't pass the test. I'm afraid that I'll get sick. I'm afraid that I won't get the job. I'm afraid that I'll be alone. I'm afraid that my child will be kidnapped.*

A few years ago I heard a news story about a woman whose newborn was taken from the hospital. The baby was soon found, unharmed. Some years later the mother had the child fingerprinted. She became obsessed with fear that her daughter would be kidnapped again. Several years after the fingerprinting, the daughter was kidnapped and killed.

The self-fulfilling prophecy of fear.

I don't understand exactly how it works, but I believe it has to do with energy and attraction—and the fact that fear expresses a component of expectation. If we think about something often, we *somehow* fuel it. We then create its reality. Our thoughts have incredible power. If we continue to focus on a specific fear, we draw the object of that fear into our consciousness. It then becomes part of our real world.

Maybe our fears and worries simply begin a cosmic process that creates energy and the *opportunity* to exist.

I dove into experiences that frightened me. I went to singles' groups to meet new men. I learned how to snowboard. I began to rock climb. I completed a twenty-three-day Outward Bound mountaineering course. My daughter and I did a sky dive from 13,000 feet. The singles group was more frightening.

Some accused me of chasing after youth. I didn't think that was what I was doing. I believed I was creating a vibrant life that would carry into my later years.

I felt young. I loved to party, to dance, to stay up late, to shoot pool and to hear the silence of new fallen snow under my board. I loved how my body felt after a workout on the climbing wall. Words cannot describe twenty-three days in the wilderness and the impact on self-esteem. Each day in the unprotected mountains provided another fear piece to move beyond. And nothing will compare to standing in front of an open airplane door, just before the jump. Each time I have that image in my mind, the most incredible smile comes over my face, followed by a surge of confidence.

I continually question: Is this direction good for me? Is this what *Hashem* wants? And when I act in a specific way or make a specific statement, I ask myself how I would feel if those words or actions became a headline on the front page of *The New York Times*. This is *my* litmus test. If I am uncomfortable with the headline I envision, I act differently. That is really hard. Something I work on daily.

I am not self-actualized. I am not problem free. I do not have all the answers. I make mistakes a lot of the time. I am not always happy. I slip and fall backward sometimes. But I am on the path, and I keep on working. I see no end in sight. That is okay. There is always another layer of unawareness to strip away. It amazes me.

I still have photographs on all of my walls. My refrigerator is covered with drawings, pictures and cartoons. Fun stuff. I have a special place for chocolate in the fridge. And two junk-food drawers. The kids are older and the conversations a bit changed, but the laughter is the same. I meditate, run, work out and affirm my goals. It all helps with the occasional sadness. Some holes just never get completely filled.

I believe when one has loved deeply, and the object of

that love is no longer present, the sadness remains. The ache lessens and most of the time there is no awareness of the loss, but every once in a while it simply grabs.

In the office, I am always asked, "When will it stop hurting?" The intensity of pain diminishes, but I have come to believe that some losses just never stop hurting. I see this as not necessarily a bad thing but fundamental to the living experience. I will never stop missing my parents. I will never stop missing my marriage. I believe the sadness honors the love I once shared.

In many ways I am a better person for my loss. I believe I am stronger, happier and much more creative. It does feel like a rebirth. I certainly look at the world through different eyes. I have a clarity I never had before. And each day gets better.

That does not mean some days don't suck, because occasionally they do. Like this morning when I thought about our log house in the mountains and how special it was on days with a blanket of soft, silent snow. But I instantly replaced that thought with an affirmation about the new mountain retreat I am going to create.

I have a resurgence of hope similar to the way I feel as I round the corner at 4th and Garfield on my morning run. When I get to that spot there is a slight downhill turn and I know I can make it the rest of the way.

I still am not sleeping on the other side of the bed, but I am under the covers these days. One night I will venture into that unknown space. When it is time. I thank God each night and each morning for all that I have.

I am so fortunate for the special people in my life, including those I work with. They allow me to touch their souls. Each day is an adventure and a celebration of life.

To be honest, I have fewer occasions when I think about the Saturday matinee of *Zardoz,* where the flying godhead chants, "The gun is good." Or the magical rainy night when Mstislav Rostropovich played an encore with the Denver Symphony to honor a friend he had lost. Or the incredible emotions experienced while watching Jimi Hendrix extract impossible sounds from his guitar.

I have accepted the significance of leading a life that honors my universe. *Paying attention is extremely important.* There must be constant awareness and a continual inventory of self.

I have also come to accept that the significant piece is not how many laws in the Torah we follow but what is in our heart as we follow them.

I believe lying is wrong. Even to a telephone solicitor. There are other ways to end a phone call. I recall Merlin in *Excalibur* saying, "When a man lies, he murders some part of the world."

Being responsible and following through with promises to others is also critical. It is so important to be someone the world trusts. It wounds *our* self-esteem when we tell someone we will arrive at 6:00 and we don't show until 6:30. And there is nothing worse than saying we will go to the movie or the dinner when we really have no intention of doing any such thing.

It is simply dishonest.

It sounds trite I know, but I want to be a good person in thought and deed. I don't want to act in ways that make me ashamed. I don't want to be dishonest with myself or the world outside my skin. I don't want to live in sadness or fear.

It's not right for me to hand those negative patterns to my child, as she will pass them directly to her child.

Different also were my responses to the man I used to call spouse. The button pushers were no longer present. Hearing his voice on the telephone did not cause an immediate physical response. Gone was that uneasy feeling in my stomach. Interactions seemed natural. Running into him was like seeing someone I used to know—a long, long time ago.

He still wants no contact, which is hurtful to our daughter—especially at celebrations such as her college graduation. Repetition of a previous time—another piece of pain for the graduate to endure.

Why can't he see that his anger toward me only assaults our daughter's essence? All she wanted on that special weekend in Maine was a picture in cap and gown—as she stood proudly between her parents. It would have been so simple.

The other day I noticed in my daughter's bedroom two black-and-white pictures together in a tiny frame—from a life long ago. She had brought the pictures back from her grandmother's house and placed the frame on her bookcase.

For a moment I was startled by what seemed like ancient images, young college graduates about to be married. I even forgot momentarily that these two people no longer had a life together. They seemed to fit so perfectly and naturally in the frame. This was my daughter's need to have her parents together again, in some small way. Even if it was just in a frame on a bookcase in a corner of her room. It meant continuity. A memory of the way it used to be. For her.

Divorce is such a forever wound to children. We don't honestly acknowledge their pain. *Their* healing takes longer—as they become skilled at coping in individual creative ways. To them survival becomes figuring out how to relate to a different, unsafe world. As they struggle with future relationships and concept of family, they come slowly to learn the meaning of trust.

29

Window of Opportunity

This process of ending a life together had its own agenda. Much of the time it was like living in a perpetual flu-fog as I waited for the virus to leave my body. I knew the trauma had to run its course, but I sometimes felt this was secret knowledge only I was privileged to possess. Folks continued with advice.

"You're taking too long. It's just a divorce."

The unaware and well-intentioned, with words that stung, had a timetable for me to follow.

Every once in a while I ran into someone who wanted to talk about what it was like for them. This did not happen often, as most people were not anxious to dredge up the past. Recently an old acquaintance said to me, "You know it took me a good five years before I felt normal again." I recall finding such affirmation in her words.

I'm pretty sure that what happens is most people simply don't deal with the loss. This is understandable considering the pressure not to. The outside world does not encourage emotional work. It is viewed as an indulgence and a weakness. This is such a misconception as incredible strength is needed to do *the work.*

Everyone wants you to get on with your life quickly, especially to be part of a couple again. But those who become involved quickly in another relationship lose the chance to work through the sadness. Such a shame, as this is a window of opportunity to learn about oneself.

Being in a vulnerable state becomes a catalyst for awareness. We gain understanding about who we are and at this time craft the necessary adjustments to our personality. *People don't make significant life changes from a place of joy.*

It's when we're hanging on by our fingernails that a paradigm shift is possible.

It is crucial to learn how to do it differently next time. We don't want those harmful childhood patterns to be repeated. You know, the ones that got us into trouble in our first marriage. But so many are quickly drawn into new relationships, believing the previous partner was the one at fault.

If one has unresolved garbage in a relationship that ends, that garbage trails along. We don't magically become garbage-free. It takes work. If we are going to have a better relationship next time, we need to find out what *our* contribution was to the failed previous relationship. Otherwise we just repeat the same negative patterns. If we had a violent temper in our first marriage, do we honestly believe that finding a new partner will do away with our awful temper?

What matters most is to *not* bury the grief. One must acknowledge the pain. As sadness ignored eventually rears its ugly head. Folks who avoid the pain (instead of confronting it) have a tendency to get old faster, become ill more often and have frequent accidents. Those who fail to do the work—pay the price. Like poisonous venom from a rattlesnake, the grief festers inside and works on the body and mind. Forever.

I nearly gave in to the pressure from the men who seemed not to understand. I came close to avoiding the process entirely. What a loss that would have been. If it were not for Reb Moshe watching out for me, or Reb Kalman's insightful concern, I would have missed the entire experience and the chance, I believe, to be free.

> The *get* provided
> a surgical finality.

As I think back to the experience in the room with the handsome man with the great tie, I can laugh now. Memory being uniquely affected by time, I can smile at the almost comedic experiences of TV cameras, telephones, maintenance men and various intruders on my most private moment. The *burial* should not have been performed on Main Street, but it was.

I could have easily become angry when the men in the room ignored me, or saddened by their attitude of indifference. It was fortunate for me that the negative aspects of the experience did not become a distraction. Not getting sucked down a black hole of negativity allowed me to remain focused.

I was able to move beyond the uncaring behavior of some who performed the ritual. I transformed their oblique energy into strength, which propelled me toward closure. Because of the ritual, I am free to experience the man who was my spouse as just a man.

I did not always understand the choices I made or the direction toward which I moved, despite the fact that I felt driven.

It seems
so obvious
now.

I stumbled upon a formula for separation and ending—a cookbook recipe.

> Add these
> ingredients
> in order
> to be
> separate and
> free.

Had I not followed the formula exactly, I would still be connected to the man and the marriage. The recipe was essential. But it was the *get* that provided the crucial vehicle for this emotional end—a finality not possible from the court alone.

30

The Power of the *Get*

When the final court papers arrived, I experienced no emotion. At the time I believed I was simply handling things well. On the other hand, I had been truly surprised by my intense grief reaction after the *get*. I learned at that time how much emotional toxicity remained within my system. The court process, however, was not the instrument for removing the toxins, the *get* was. In order to heal, the negative emotions had to be purged.

The *get* sliced into me and pierced my soul. The experience was reminiscent of reaching for the shovel at an Orthodox funeral. Nothing is more final than the sound of dirt hitting a pine box. The purpose is not morbidity but pure genius. The goal is simple: Bring the emotions to the surface in a profound way.

The *get* is an intense adventure, not an insignificant encounter. It is wrong that women fear the process and are discouraged from participation. Yet often this is the sad reality, as the *get* becomes an overwhelming experience that is both frightening and humiliating.

The *get* is a powerful ritual that should honor both the man and the woman in their quest for an end. Nothing within the process should resemble waiting in the grocery checkout line. Yet there were those elements, as the line began to form slowly behind me.

The problem seems to be that many who seek the *get* appear interested not in the process but in the tangible document required to fulfill the law. This is sad. The *get* is much more than twelve black lines on a piece of white parchment.

Why should a unique spiritual process with profound potential for healing be experienced by men as nonessential and by women as condescending?

It is such a

waste.

The *get* should be conducted in a spiritual manner that honors Torah and the ancient ritual. Specifically, it is this act of honoring that facilitates the release of negative energy from the bowels of the relationship.

The discharge of this energy is *crucial* to transformation.

And it is this *transformation of energy* that allows the relationship to die.

When a relationship ends without true closure, the residual toxic energy intensifies the old connection. This causes the relationship to live on and, simply, to never end.

Possibly this persistent negative energy and the lack of finality could account for the increased number of high-conflict divorces that continue without resolution. Anger and bitterness become the fuel that *strengthen* the connection, long after the marriage has ended.

> The *get* can
> transform
> this energy and
> dissolve
> the connection . . .
> forever.

Our culture encourages elaborate wedding ceremonies for couples who have known each other a short time and may have never even touched. Yet most of the time we have no dissolution ceremony for two people who have created children and experienced a lifetime together.

A meaningful ceremony marking the end of a life together honors the relationship and provides the necessary psychological end.

Part of the prescription for healing was following the exact recipe and making sure to carefully add every ingredient. I had to do it all, even when I did not understand. This was about jumping with eyes closed—a definite leap of faith.

The memories fade—of playing Thumper at the Sink in Boulder as we downed beers and patiently etched our names into worn tables soaked with history. Distant are thoughts of brilliant reds and yellows—a panoply of cover rustling across our path as we walked so slowly and made promises we did not keep.

I am beginning to feel like my flu-head has lifted. There are fewer moments when I am sad, and on many days I feel incredibly happy. I survived and transcended the pain of a monumental loss. I see myself beginning a new stage of existence—filled with gratitude and optimism for life.

Without my *recipe* I would be stuck forever in anger, resentment and sadness—still tied to the man. The *get* provided the instrument for separation, an ancient formula for a profound end. A gift from *Hashem*.

EPILOGUE

You might remember the other boy, the one my father expected me to marry. Well, we did lose contact. But what I never knew was that he saved a picture of me, placed it in his dresser drawer and left it there—for thirty years.

A while ago, he wrote me. It was quite a surprise. I noticed his letter in the morning mail at the office but saved it to read in the evening—in bed. The letter was pretty short, less than a page and not real informative. It asked one question.

How about dinner
in Boulder
one night?

What happened next
is *really*
another story
for another
time.
I promise.

ABOUT THE AUTHOR

Elise Edelson Katch, L.C.S.W., has been a practicing therapist, evaluator, educator, expert witness and consult-ant for the past twenty-five years in Denver, Colorado. She specializes in the fields of trauma and high-conflict divorce, and works as a Special Advocate to the courts. She holds a B.A. in the social sciences and an M.A. in reading educa-tion from the University of Colorado, as well as an M.S.W. from the University of Denver. The American Professional Society on the Abuse of Children has recognized her for outstanding achievement in the field of child abuse and neglect. Elise helped to craft the first child custody guidelines in Colorado, and was the founder and first president of the Colorado Professional Society on the Abuse of Children. She is a past treasurer of the National Association of Counsel for Children. She has been published in the *Colorado Lawyer* and provides expert testimony in Colorado and nationally. Elise presents seminars and lectures on parent–child relationships and divorce-related matters. She is an active member of the Metropolitan Denver Interdisciplinary Committee—an organization composed of attorneys, mental health professionals and judges working together in the field of divorce. She has been an adjunct professor at the University of Denver Graduate School of Social Work, as well as a presenter at the Colorado Psychological Association and the Breckenridge Child Custody Conference. Often quoted in the print media, Elise has done television interviews, both locally and nationally.